Keep Your Friends Close and Your Enemies Closer: Operational Design for a Nuclear-Armed Iran

School of Advanced Military Studies
United States Army Command and General Staff College
Fort Leavenworth, Kansas

Abstract

Keeping Your Friends Close and Your Enemies Closer: Operational Design for a Nuclear-Armed Iran by MAJOR Robert K. Umstead, USAF, 62 pages.

The Islamic Republic of Iran (IRI) has pursued a nuclear program since 1985. In February 2006, with the last round of international negotiations having failed and International Atomic Energy Agency (IAEA) having reported the dossier to the United Nations Security Council, Tehran is on the precipice of being able to field a nuclear weapon at a time convenient to the IRI. A nuclear-armed Iran will change the strategic calculus in the Middle East and Central Asia and present new risks to US interests in the region. This monograph will address the issue of a nuclear-armed Iran from four perspectives; historical patterns of Iranian behavior with respect to foreign influence, a western perspective of these patterns, a technical review of Iran's nuclear program, and a methodology called systemic operational design (SOD).

SOD is an application of systems theory to operational art that focuses on the relationships between the entities within a system to translate strategic direction and policy into an operational design. This systemic approach, synthesizes the Iranian historical pattern of balancing one foreign power with another while simultaneously seeking to limit foreign influence with the Western perspectives of international politics and the technical realities of Iran's nuclear program. A design that seeks to "keep our friends close and our enemies closer" by simultaneously pursuing economic growth and regional stability through reopening of the US embassy in Iran while disrupting the foreign networks that support the proliferation of nuclear technology along with those that finance and support the foreign activities of Iran's IRGC and Hezbollah provides an initial frame and direction for action to manage the risks posed by a nuclear-armed Iran.

TABLE OF CONTENTS

TABLE OF FIGURES

INTRODUCTION

The Islamic Republic of Iran (IRI) has pursued a nuclear program since 1985. In February 2006, with the last round of international negotiations having failed and International Atomic Energy Agency (IAEA) having reported the dossier to the United Nations Security Council[1], Tehran is on the precipice of being able to field a nuclear weapon at a time convenient to the IRI. A nuclear-armed Iran will change the strategic calculus in the Middle East and Central Asia and present new risks to US interests in the region. The National Strategy for Combating Terrorism identifies Iran as one of the seven state sponsors of terrorism.[2] Further, according to the National Security Strategy any state sponsor of terrorism that attempts to gain weapons of mass destruction requires immediate attention.[3] A policy of "just say no" is difficult to execute. In fact, the nuclear genie may already be out of the bottle in Iran. The question then, is not "How do we keep Iran from fielding a nuclear weapon," but "How do we manage the risks posed by Iran when they field a nuclear weapon?"

This monograph will address the issue of a nuclear-armed Iran from four perspectives; historical patterns of Iranian behavior with respect to foreign influence, a western perspective of these patterns, a technical review of Iran's nuclear program, and a methodology called systemic operational design. Beginning with a review of Persian/Iranian history, the context of Persian glory followed by foreign dominance is used to develop and to illustrate a pattern of balancing one foreign power with another while simultaneously attempting to rid Iran of foreign influence.

Second, to gain insight into Iran's intentions, this historical pattern along with Iran's more recent activity in the nuclear arena will be reviewed through the Western theoretical perspectives of international relations of realism, liberalism, and idealism. While the generation of electricity is a valid use of nuclear power, a nuclear program also enables Iran to counter

---

[1] Associated Press. "Iran to Resume Nuke Program in Face of Referral to UN Security Council," 4 February 2006. www.foxnews.com, accessed 4 February 2005.
[2] *National Strategy for Combating Terrorism*. February 2003
[3] *The National Security Strategy of the United States of America*. September 2002

perceived threats and attain regional power status. Third, stating a desire to master nuclear technology is one thing but fielding a nuclear weapon is another. An open source review of Iran's nuclear program suggests it may be too late to prevent Iran from fielding a nuclear weapon if it decides to do so.

Finally, a methodology called Systemic Operational Design (SOD) is utilized to synthesize the Iranian historical pattern of balancing one foreign power with another while simultaneously seeking to limit foreign influence with the Western perspectives of international politics and the technical realities of Iran's nuclear program. SOD is an application of systems theory to operational art that focuses on the relationships between the entities within a system to translate strategic direction and policy into an operational design. Through this systemic approach, the strategic calculus and risks of a nuclear-armed Iran will be assessed and a direction for action proposed.

HISTORICAL BACKGROUND

At one time, the territory of Persia extended from Egypt to the mountains of Afghanistan. In 480 B.C., the Persian Empire was the global superpower. Iran has been the only predominantly Shi'i Muslim state in the world for five centuries. Nevertheless, in the early 1800s Persia was a weak state caught between two new superpowers engaged in The Great Game, Britain and Russia.[4] For about 150 years, Persia was both battleground and a source of natural resources, primarily petroleum, for the Europeans, Russia, and later the United States. This sharp reversal of fortune and the resultant desire to limit or eliminate foreign influence is still relevant today in the context of the nuclear ambitions of the Islamic Republic of Iran. To develop this context, a review of Iranian history is in order.

---

[4] Groseclose, Elgin. *Introduction to Iran.* New York: Oxford University Press, 1947, p.127.

In about 612 B.C. the Persians, together with the Babylonians, defeated the Assyrians and sacked the Assyrian capital of Ninevah signaling the beginnings of a Persian expansion.[5] In 559 B.C. Cyrus II took the Persian throne and expanded the Persian territory north into what is the center of present day Iran as well as to the east before turning west. By 546 B.C., Cyrus' armies conquered territory from the Aegean Coast of Asia Minor to the Hindu Kush.[6] He then turned south to conquer Babylon in 539 B.C. Cyrus' son Cambyses II added Egypt.[7] When Darius I took the throne in 522 B.C., the Persian Empire extended from Afghanistan to Mediterranean.

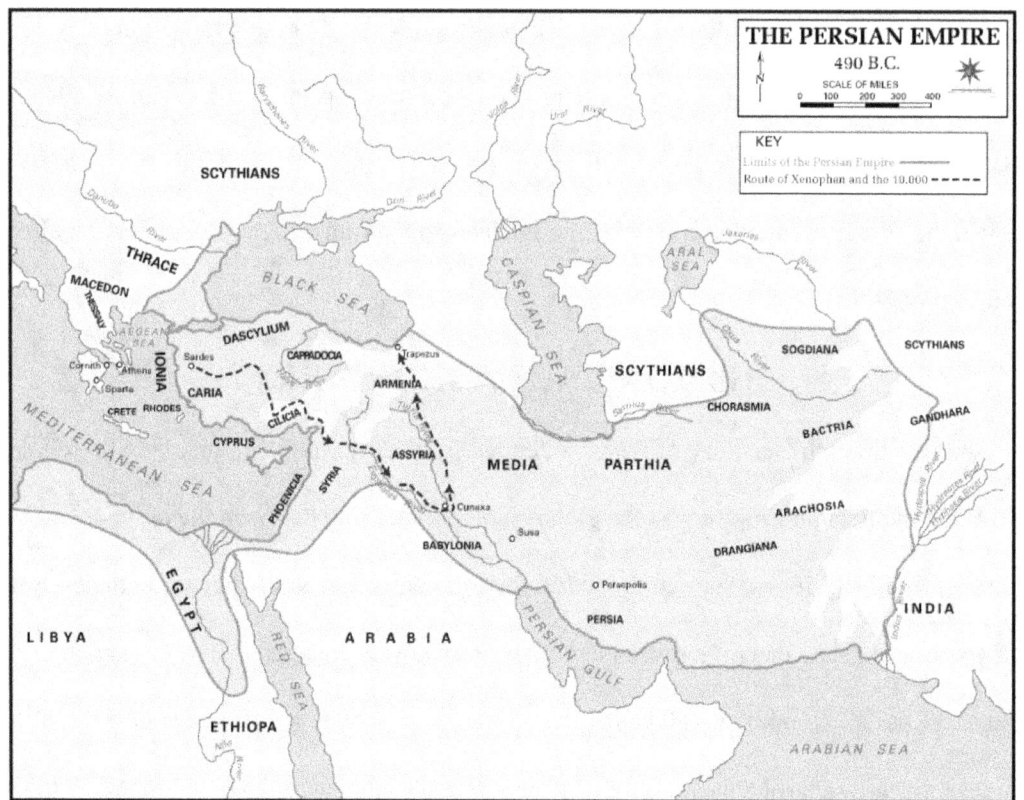

Figure 1: Persian Empire 490 B.C.[8]

[5] Pollack, Kenneth M. *The Persian Puzzle, the Conflict between Iran and America.* New York: random House Trade Paperback Edition, 2005, p. 7.

[6] Metz, Helen Chapin, Editor. *Iran, a Country Study.* Washington, D.C.: Federal Research Division, Library of Congress, 1989, p. 6.

[7] Frye, Richard N. *The Heritage of Persia.* Cleveland: The World Publishing Company, 1963, pp. 78, 84.

[8] Created by the Department of History, United States Military Academy, West Point. http://www.dean.usma.edu/departments/history/atlases/ancient_warfare/persian_empire_490bc.html, accessed 5 March 2006.

Darius ruled through provincial governors, built roads, developed a monetary system, and the Persian economy dominated the region. He also invaded Greece. In 490 B.C., Darius landed at Marathon but ultimately the Athenians prevail. His son Xerxes led a much larger force in 480 B.C. A Xerxes force suffered the famous defeat at Thermopylae at the hands of the Spartans but was not ultimately defeated for another year by a combined Greek force.[9] This defeat marked the end of the expansion of the Persian Empire, but the decline did not begin in earnest for another 150 years with the coming of Alexander the Great.

In 334 B.C., Alexander the Great conquered the greatest superpower the world had seen. He defeated the Persian Army at Arbela in modern day northern Iraq in 331 and occupied the Persian capital of Persepolis the next year. However, Alexander died in 323 and the empire divided between his generals. In 224 A.D., the Sassanids would win the struggle for power and rule Iran and Mesopotamia for 400 years until unseated by a new power, Islam.[10]

The Sassanids developed a highly centralized state but fought many wars to maintain the empire in the east and against the Romans in the west. By the sixth century, the Sassanids had begun to weaken and suffered many internal revolts. Five years after the Arabian Peninsula had fallen to Islamic armies in 632, victory over the Sassanids at Qadisiyah led to control of Mesopotamia. The Sassanids ultimately fell at Nahavand in 642.[11] Iran remained in the Islamic empires through the tenth and eleventh centuries. Climatic changes leading to desertification and forcing much of the population to adopt a more nomadic way of life made the region hard to govern centrally. It also made the population vulnerable to invasion by tribes from central Asia. Without question, the most devastating of these were the Mongol invasions that began in the thirteenth century. The Mongols were exceptionally good at destruction. Combined with a second invasion in the fourteenth century the Mongols destroyed many of the cities including

---

[9] Metz, pp. 6-7.
[10] Metz, pp. 9-10.
[11] Frye, pp. 202-231.

Shiraz and Isfahan and radically altered the demography of Iran by massacring many Iranian males. The instability left by the Mongols presented an opportunity for Afghan and Turkic tribes to fight over Iran. However, an indigenous group who would bring the Shi'i version of Islam to Iran, the Safavids, would finally reunify the country for the first time in a millennium. The Safavids ruled for two centuries.[12]

The Safavid Empire ended in 1722 when tribesmen from Afghanistan invaded and took control of much of Iran ushering in another phase of power struggles between both internal and external powers. Finally, in 1795 a tribe known as the Qajars defeated the other tribes and managed to reunify the country.[13] Unfortunately for the Qajars, the world outside Persia was changing fast and not in an advantageous way. The rise of oceangoing trade hurt the mountain trade routes and the increasing nomadic nature of the population continued to make centralized government difficult. Russia and the European states were growing stronger and the British East India Company gained rights to trading post at Bushehr in 1763. The Great Game was just getting started, with Persia caught in the middle.[14]

The first war with the Russians began in 1804 in present day Georgia. After a nine-year fight, Persia ceded rights to all lands in the Caucasus and gave up the right to a navy on the Caspian Sea. The defeat only served to increase British interest in the country. Given the recent defeat, convincing the Persian shah (king) to sign a protectorate agreement with Britain was relatively easy. While the shah hoped to regain lands lost to the Russians, the British were interested in protecting Indian trade routes. A Persian army strong enough to threaten Russia was potentially strong enough to threaten India and not in the interests of Britain.[15]

Thus began over 150 years of back and forth between Persian/Iranian agreements with one outside power to counter another. In the end, the only losers were the Iranians. Each swing

---

[12] Metz, pp. 15-16.
[13] Metz, pp. 19-20.
[14] Pollack, p. 14.
[15] Ibid.

of the pendulum from one power to the next would lead to resentment of foreign meddling, but during the Great Game Persia's strategic position next to Afghanistan and India ensured foreign interest.[16] In the 1900s, two world wars and oil drove the foreign interest. Today the cycle continues; Russia, Britain, and India are still involved. Relatively new players include the United States, China and the European Union. Oil, natural gas, and trade are the familiar drivers of foreign interest; the newcomer is the potential for nuclear weapons.

The shah did attempt to regain the Caucasus lands in 1826. However, at the time, the British and Russians allied against the Turks in the War of Greek Independence. As a result, the British did not assist the Shah. The Russians trounced the Persian army and forced the shah to sign the Treaty of Turkmanchai confirming the loss of lands in the Caucasus, granting economic concessions and promising reparations.[17]

Compounding the Persian military problems were the continued climatic and economic changes as well as internal corruption. Desertification, growth in European manufacturing, continued growth in maritime trade and problems of communication across the Persian countryside all continued to weaken the nation throughout the 1800s. Government ministers and the shahs spent money freely and without regard for the needs of the state. The Qajars began to borrow money to pay for everything from attempted reforms to wars to several month trips to Europe. Combined with the weakening economy, this pattern of borrowing only made Persia more reliant on the Europeans.

These economic and corruption problems were epitomized in The Reuter Concession of 1872. The shah, needing cash, granted Baron Paul Julius von Reuter a monopoly over almost all of Persia's economic and financial resources. The agreement was so unpopular the shah canceled

---

[16] Pakistan did not exist in 1814.
[17] Metz, p. 20.

it after only one year.[18] The episode was a harbinger of things to come. A large percentage of Persians now had a significant split with the government and the government still needed cash.

The discontent surfaced in 1891 during the Tobacco Revolt. The regime, by then desperate for money, granted a tobacco concession to a Briton for a monopoly on all tobacco sold in Persia. Tobacco, widely grown and smoked by Persians, promised high profits for the monopoly but higher prices for consumers and lower profits for Persian farmers and merchants. A fatwa, or religious ruling, forbidding smoking issued by a leading cleric was widely observed. The shah canceled the concession with a payoff to Imperial Tobacco pushing the government further into debt.[19]

The events of 1891 focused public opinion against foreign concessions, viewed as meddling, and undermined the British position in Persia. Additionally, the revolt demonstrated that the various groups within the society had a common interest, nationalism, and could change the course of events if they united. Finally, the Tobacco Revolt demonstrated a divide between the regime and the rest of society. These splits between the regime and society along with the spirit of nationalism have persisted and have been important to the context of Iranian behavior to this day.

The Americans arrived in the Persian Gulf in the early 1800s. By the 1850s trade between the United States and the Gulf countries had grown enough the Americans negotiated the Treaty of Friendship and Commerce with Persia in 1856 despite British efforts to prevent it. Similar to the way they had courted the British to counter the Russians the Persians, the Persians began to court the Americans to balance the perceived threat from the British. The United States opened a diplomatic mission in Tehran in 1883.[20]

---

[18] Yapp, M.E. *The Making of the Modern Near East, 1792-1923*. New York: Longman, Inc., 1987, p. 166.
[19] Metz, p. 22.
[20] Pollack, p. 19.

The turn of the century brought the return of the Russians as well as two fateful deals, one with Russia and one with Britain. In 1900-1902, the Persians secured large loans from Russia.[21] At the same time, the Persians granted William K. D'Arcy a 60-year concession for the rights to oil exploration throughout Persia except on the border with Russia in return for just 16 percent of the profits.[22]

A move against the regime similar to that of the Tobacco Revolt quickly developed. The demands of the various groups gelled around the conclusion Persia needed a constitutional democracy. The idea was to create a government that could control the shah's ability to sell off the country's resources for the personal gain of himself and his ministers. In December of 1906, the shah signed the new constitution ending the first round in the Constitutional Revolution. Victory was, however, short lived. The coalition that united behind nationalist interests began to come apart. Additionally, the relationship between Persia, Russia, and Britain fundamentally changed in 1907 when Britain and Russia signed the Anglo-Russian Agreement ending the Great Game and turning their interests toward the rising Germany.[23]

Part of the Anglo-Russian agreement carved up Persia into three areas of influence. The Russians would control the northern region of Persia, Britain the southern portion, and the Persians the central portion. The two countries granted themselves the rights to sign agreements and apportion revenues from the Persian government to pay off Persian loans. Naturally, none of this was favorable to the Persians and the years from 1908 – 1911 saw the return of the shah followed by a return of the constitutionalists. By 1911, the British and Russians were actively undermining efforts by the Americans, all on Persian soil. The Russians invaded the north, again. The British invaded the south. Russia demanded the dismissal of the American economic advisor

---

[21] Ibid, p. 23.
[22] Pollack, p. 20.
[23] Metz, pp. 23-24.

contracted by the Persian government. When the Persian parliament (the Majles) refused, tribal chiefs dissolved it by force and the Persian democracy came to and end.[24]

While the Great Game had ended, foreign influence in Persia had not and the attempted balancing by reaching out to America only served to agitate Russia and Britain against Persia. The Constitutional Revolution cemented the concept of an independent Persia without foreign domination (nationalism) in the minds of Persians. Based on current rhetoric surrounding Iran's nuclear program, this theme rings as true in 2006 as it did in 1911.

World War I did not help the Persian situation and foreign interest, particularly British interest, only increased when William D'Arcy struck oil in 1908. The Royal Navy had switched to oil burning ships in 1911 so this find was critical on the eve of war. Persian oil was so important to the Royal Navy; the British government acquired a 51 percent share in the Anglo-Persian Oil Company (APOC). In 1915, Britain secretly agreed to a treaty with the Russians to grant them control of the Turkish Strait and Istanbul in return for British control over the central zone of Persia (previously "given" to the Persians in the Anglo-Russia agreement of 1907) where the oilfields were.[25] By the end of WWI Persia was once again a battleground with the Ottomans, Russians, and British all present on Persian territory. Central government authority broke down completely; widespread tribal raiding and famine were common.[26]

By wars end the British had the advantage due in large part to Russia's communist revolution. In 1919, London and Tehran signed the Anglo-Persian Agreement making Persia a protectorate (again). The agreement gave Britain exclusive rights to training the Persian Army, build infrastructure, and revise the tariff system. In return, Britain provided a loan and significant financial inducements for the Iranian prime minister and two members of the cabinet.[27] Once again, nationalism took hold when the Majles refused to ratify the treaty and the Azerbaijanis

---

[24] Ibid.
[25] Pollack, p. 24.
[26] Yapp, p. 288.
[27] Metz, p. 25.

declared an independent republic in 1920. Britain moved forward regardless, modifying the tariff laws and taking over the Army. However, over the next year Britain concluded things were too out of hand and withdrew all her troops by the end of 1921 leaving a dysfunctional Persian government.

After a little over a hundred years, the back and forth pattern of foreign influence in Persia was well established. Persian efforts to rid itself of this foreign presence only led to continued foreign presence. By the end of WWI, the Persian Empire had fallen very far indeed. A hundred years of weakness and domination by foreign powers left an indelible impression on Persian foreign policy; end foreign influence in Persia.[28]

Reza Khan was the commander of the Cossack Division in what was left of the Persian Army. He seized power in February of 1921 in a coup d'etat. He became prime minister in 1923 and the Majles appointed him shah in 1925. He named himself Reza Shah Pahlavi. His broad objective, like many Persian leaders before him, was to diminish, or better yet eliminate, foreign influence in his country.[29]

The new Shah began quickly in 1921 when Persia signed a treaty with the USSR that led to the withdrawal of Soviet forces from the northern part of the country and the forgiveness of all debts and claims owed to the now deposed Russian Tsar. Reza Shah then set aside the Anglo-Persian agreement of 1919, but asked British advisors to remain and assist with reorganizing the government.[30] For all his desire to lower the foreign influence in his kingdom, Reza Shah had followed the same path many of his predecessors had. He balanced one or more foreign powers with another. The Shah's new government reached to America to counter the influence of Britain and the Soviets. The new government offered oil concessions but the deals were quickly killed

---

[28] Pollack, pp. 25-26.
[29] Lenczowski, George, editor. *Iran under the Pahlavis.* Stanford: Hoover Institution Press, 1978, pp. 12-27.
[30] Pollack, p. 29.

by either Soviet or British protests. Finally, Persia and America signed a new commercial agreement in 1928.

While inviting foreign commercial involvement from the Americans and distancing himself from the Soviets, Reza Shah still had a problem with the British: the Anglo-Persian Oil Company. The agreement between the Persian government and the company had never been favorable to the Persians. After the Majles refused to support a new deal in 1927, the shah instituted an income tax of four percent, which APOC refused to pay. In 1932, the shah simply canceled the concession. This move brought APOC to the bargaining table and a new agreement was signed in 1933 that returned most of the territory in the original agreement (APOC retained the territory where oil had been discovered) and improving Tehran's oil revenues.[31] Having temporarily satiated his desire to lower foreign influence in Persia, the shah turned to consolidating his power internally.

From 1921 through 1930 the shah used a consolidated army, now free of British and Russian officers, to reassert the control of the central government to the tribal and provincial society that had come to pass.[32] He moved into areas of northern Persia and filled the vacuum left by the departure of the Soviets. He brought revolts by Kurdish, Turkoman, and Azerbaijani movements under control and moved south to solidify Persian rule over the oil rich province of Khuzestan. Finally, by 1930, he had brought the tribes of eastern and southern Iran under control through annual campaigns, negotiation or both.[33] The invigoration of the Persian Army and consequently the ability of the shah to centralize his power were due in no small part to the increase in oil revenue.

This oil revenue also enabled the shah to modernize and industrialize Iran (in 1935 he began to call the country Iran vice Persia). These efforts included roads, telephone lines, and a

---

[31] Groseclose, pp. 140-141.
[32] Yapp, M.E. *The Near East since the First World War.* New York: Longman, Inc. 1991 p.160-187.
[33] Lenczowski, pp. 21-22, 29.

railroad that connected the Caspian ports to the ports on the Persian Gulf. Additionally, a new legal code based on the French system and a variety of financial reforms including a central bank took effect. Finally, the shah put it place new commercial agreements including higher tariffs, an expanded education system including the establishment of Tehran University, expanded industrial production, programs, and a state bureaucracy to manage it all.[34]

While these programs were extensive, not everybody in Iran benefited. The agricultural sector stagnated. Further, the shah was not exactly open to democracy. By rigging elections, outlawing political parties and generally intimidating opponents he quickly alienated the constitutional reformists. The clergy were unhappy with the secular nature of the shah's government, with new governmental control over religious endowments, and with a new requirement to pass a government test to receive a license to practice their religion.[35] In sum, while the shah had managed to reduce the level of foreign influence in Iran by the end of the 1930s he was deeply unpopular in many sectors of Iranian society.

One of these sectors, however, was not the large landowners. The large property owners owning one or more villages and receiving rent from the agricultural laborers controlled "local" Iranian society. Under Reza Shah, these landowners benefited from sales of state land and the removal of a land tax in 1934. The shah became the largest landowner in Iran. While the number of clerics in the Majles had steadily declined in the 1920s, the number of landowners increased. The Pahlavi regime was a landowner regime.[36] Indeed, the relationship between the shah, the clergy (who also owned significant amounts of land) and the large landowners would eventually play a significant role in the downfall of the Pahlavi dynasty. However, in the 1930s, the power rested with the landowners and Reza Shah adopted a conciliatory approach.

---

[34] Ibid, pp. 29-35.
[35] Metz, p. 26.
[36] Yapp, p. 175.

As the winds of war began to strengthen, the shah's time in power was likely coming to an end. The benefits of hindsight show he had upset much of society, including the clergy, the agricultural workers and *bazaaris*. However, Reza Shah's fate would not be decided in Iran but in Europe. As World War II began, Iran could not afford to alienate Britain, Germany, or the Soviet Union. Nevertheless, the war sapped the supply of goods the shah's plans depended upon and crippled the economy. When Germany invaded Russia, the shah's objective of minimizing foreign influence in Iran was doomed. The combination of oil, a railroad from the Persian Gulf to the Caspian, and the shah's refusal to dismiss the Germans working in Iran was not something the Allies could ignore. In August 1941 the British and Soviets demanded the ports be made available and any Germans in Iran be sent home. Naturally, the shah refused. Britain and Russia invaded, crushed the Iranian army in less than two weeks, the shah's government collapsed and Iran was once again dominated by foreign powers. The shah went into exile and the Allies installed his son Mohammad Reza on the throne. Although dominated by the Allied occupying forces during the war, Mohammad Reza Shah Pahlavi would adopt a similar policy to that of his father and other predecessors; minimize foreign influence in Iran and increase Iran's power and independence.[37]

The Allied occupation of Iran from 1941-1946 was legalized by a three party treaty in September 1941 in which the occupying powers promised to respect Iran's territorial integrity, independence, sovereignty, and to leave within six months of the end of the war.[38] In 1942, the United States also entered into an agreement with Iran. In due course, 30,000 Americans would run the Lend-Lease supply lines from the Persian Gulf to the Caspian Sea. Up to 34 percent of the Lend-Lease, supplies to Russia would transit through Iran in 1943 and by wars end 26 percent

---

[37] Pollack, pp. 37-39.
[38] Groseclose, pp. 173-174.

of the total Lend-Lease aid would have traveled through Iran. While the Americans ran the supply lines, the Soviets took up positions in the north, the British in the south.[39]

The war was a disaster for Iranian society placing demands on the local economy far in excess of what it could handle. Inflation and food shortages were rampant.[40] The Pahlavi regime did not fare much better. Most of the Pahlavi lands were taken by the state, the army was crushed (and what remained could not be freely used by the shah due to the occupation), and the new shah, Mohammad Reza Shah, could no longer control the Majles. Instead, the shah traded space for time and focused on control of the army so he could restore the regime after the war.

As with the Anglo-Russian agreement in 1907, the occupying powers did not exactly live up to their promises. In 1944, the Soviets in northern Iran demanded a concession for oil as well as mineral deposits along with the rights to exploit these deposits. The Majles refused and eventually passed a law prohibiting any Iranian official from negotiating an oil agreement with another state. In 1945, rather than withdraw the Soviets provided aid to Azerbaijani separatists and blocked Iranian army forces when they tried to regain control. The British and Americans had left Iran by March of 1946. The Soviets, however, stayed. While Washington and Moscow maneuvered in an early Cold War crisis, Iran reached an agreement with the Soviets. In return for an oil concession in the north, the Soviets would withdraw by the end of May 1946, contingent on Majles approval. The Soviets departed, but the Majles rejected the concession in October 1947. The departure of the Soviets allowed the shah to regain control of the Northern provinces as well as return Iranian borders to the pre-World War II status.[41] However, as with his predecessors dating back to the mid 1800s the shah still needed money.

The only source of this money was oil. The shah approached the United States for aid -- rather than Russia or Britain -- but was disappointed with the results. Therefore, a renegotiation

---

[39] Pollack, pp. 40-41.
[40] Groseclose, pp. 183.
[41] Ibid, pp. 230-242.

of the Anglo-Iranian oil concession was needed. Here the shah would run headlong into internal political dissent. The shah signed an agreement but the Majles declined and called for a national oil company. At this point oil was no longer simply a commodity, it was a symbol of independence.

Independence was a common theme in the Iranian energy industry after World War II and still is today. Iran claims nuclear power is necessary to produce electricity so that oil and natural gas can be put on the international market and ensure cash flow into the economy. However, Iran today is once again between independence and foreign influence. In an effort to gain "energy independence" Iran has signed oil and natural gas development deals with China, Japan, and three European companies as well as an agreement with Russia for nuclear reactors.[42] In 1946, the Iranian government reached out to the Americans to balance the influence of Russia and Britain. Today it is China, Japan, and Russia to balance the perceived threat of the Americans, and the issue still revolves around oil and independence.

In response to the Majles vote, the shah appointed a new prime minister to ram the deal through, but the prime minister was assassinated in March 1951. In November 1950, Saudi Arabia and the Americans agreed on a fifty-fifty split within ARAMCO, the conglomerate operating in Saudi Arabia. This agreement put additional pressure on Britain to match the deal, but the British Foreign Office rejected it. Additionally, there was now public unrest over the new concession. Faced with this public pressure, the Majles voted in March 1951 to nationalize the oil industry. The shah, under pressure from the Majles, named Mohammad Mosaddeq prime minister a month later.[43] Mosaddeq had two broad goals, independence and the extension of democracy. Oil nationalization, therefore, was as much a political issue as an economic one and

---

[42] de Bellaigue, Christopher. "Iran" *Foreign Policy*, May/June 2005. Washington, D.C.: Carnegie Endowment for International Peace, 2005. p. 19. AFP. "Japan to Develop Iran Oilfield." *AlJazeera.net*, www.english.aljazeera.net, accessed 15 February 2006. Reuters. "Iran in Gas Deal with European Firms." *AlJazeera.net*, www.english.aljazeera.net, accessed 25 February 2006
[43] Metz, pp. 29-30.

the option of reaching a new concession with the Anglo-Iranian Oil Company was simply not acceptable.[44] Ultimately, he would fail on both counts. The British response was to draw up plans to seize the oil fields with 70,000 troops, freeze Iranian assets in British banks, prohibit export of British goods to Iran, and use the Royal Navy to blockade Iranian oil exports. AIOC shut down the oilfields and convinced all the international oil firms not to purchase Iranian oil, a move greatly aided by an excess of oil supply at the time.[45]

Mosaddeq's reasons for being obstinate are unclear. One possible explanation; he was using the issue to weaken the shah. Another is he thought America would step in to offset the threat of communism. Still another is he thought Iran would be able to sell the oil by itself and could therefore become free of foreign meddling. In the fall of 1952, the Americans pressed hard for an AIOC deal. The British agreed to a fifty-fifty split of the AIOC profits, but Mosaddeq turned the offer down and instead demanded reparations for lost oil revenue. In the meantime, he hinted to the new administration in Washington he would turn to the Soviets if he did not get what he wanted. These two decisions sealed his fate. Internal Iranian politics were equally intense and Mosaddeq was equally obstinate. Finally, on 19 August 1953, the army overthrew Mosaddeq with the assistance of MI6 and the CIA.[46] The oil issue was finally resolved in 1954 with an agreement that gave Iran control of its oil resources. Oil production was divided between a group of foreign firms including several American firms, Royal Dutch Shell and the renamed AIOC, British Petroleum. As a result, Iranian oil revenue grew steadily from less than $100 million in 1955 to nearly $500 million in 1964.[47]

The oil nationalization crisis may provide some insight to the current crisis over Iran's nuclear program. The Iranian government has steadfastly been unwilling to make a deal in the

---

[44] Katouzian, Homa. "Mosaddeq's Government in Iranian History, Arbitrary Rule, Democracy, and the 1953 Coup." *Mohammad Mosaddeq and the 1953 Coup in Iran.* Gasiorowski, Mark J. and Byrne, Malcom, editors. Syracuse: Syracuse University Press, 2004, pp. 4-5.

[45] Pollack, pp. 56-57.

[46] Katouzian, p. 18.

[47] Pollack, p. 75.

nuclear arena, even though they have been willing to negotiate. The reasons for this unwillingness are as unclear as Mosaddeq's obstinacy. Is Iranian nationalism or factional internal politics to blame? A desire to appear strong in the face of foreign "bullying"? Dislike of the Americans in the same manner Mosaddeq disliked the British? Is it all of the above? Certainly, Mosaddeq miscalculated when it came to how the British and particularly the Americans would act. For their part, the British likely miscalculated with respect to Mosaddeq's actions. The result was the overthrow of the Iranian government by Britain and the United States.

Today both sides, the Iranians and the international community led by the EU-3, have come to an impasse. The IAEA has reported Iran to the United Nations Security Council for violating its responsibilities under the Non-Proliferation Treaty. Similarly, the Iranians have continued to press ahead announcing they would restart their dormant nuclear program in the face of interventional pressure and referring to American leaders as "terrorists and the main axis of evil in the world."[48] While overthrow of the Iranian government does not appear imminent, the current situation is eerily similar to 1952 – 1953. Certainly, the Iranians with over 150 years of being preoccupied with foreign influence in the country will not have forgotten.

Through the remainder of the 1960s and into the mid-1970s, the shah increased his hold on power and Iran effectively became a dictatorship. Iran changed economically and demographically very quickly between 1960 and 1979. The money for economic growth came from oil. The "White Revolution" and would change Iran from an agricultural economy to an industrial one. It would also alienate the shah from his primary power base, the landowners. Whereas Reza Shah had been conciliatory to the landowners, his son followed a path to land reform that forced landowners to sell land to the state. This effectively broke the power of the families who controlled Iran's agricultural economy. The result changed the face of the Majles with far fewer landowners being elected and the shah losing influence over the body. Land

[48] Associated Press. "Iran to Resume Nuke Program in Face of Referral to UN Security Council." www.foxnews.com, accessed 4 February 2005.

reform also alienated the clergy by taking away the wealth of the religious community and hurting village property owners who were the most important to the mullahs. The shah retained his power by increasingly repressive means. Internally unrest began to swirl in the late 1960s and into the 1970s, the clergy being the primary agitator.[49]

The "Two-Pillars" strategy of the Nixon administration, while it served American interests by using the proxies of Saudi Arabia and Iran to maintain stability in the Persian Gulf, only heightened the sense of American influence over the shah among ordinary Iranians. For his part, the shah used much of the oil revenue to buy military equipment from the Americans. However, when the oil crisis of the mid-1970s hit the shah fanned the flames and convinced OPEC to raise oil prices again in December 1973, hardly the work of an American puppet.[50]

The economic boom ended in 1976. Recession in the West ultimately brought the price of oil down but the Iranian government had been spending a great deal of money. Inflation, unemployment and disappointment led to protest in 1977. In 1977, a cycle of street demonstrations and riots began. In September of 1978, the demonstrations turned into strikes bringing industry, the oil industry in particular, to a halt. The shah fled in January 1979. On February 1, 1979, Ayatollah Ruhollah Musavi Khomeini returned to Iran and the Islamic Republic of Iran (IRI) was born.[51]

It is against this historical backdrop, combined with the Iran-Iraq war and years of what the West considered state-sponsored terrorism, the current saga between Iran and its various foreign interlocutors continues to play out. The memories of Persian glory may be distant, but are nonetheless real. The paradox of balancing one foreign power with another while simultaneously ridding Iran of foreign influence is as real in 2006 as it was in 1804. The issues are familiar ones, oil and independence. This time the balancing mechanism is nuclear energy. Generating power

---

[49] Yapp, pp. 334-343.
[50] Pollack, pp. 103-107.
[51] Metz, pp. 43-47.

by mastering nuclear technology means more oil is available for state revenue and the state is less reliant on foreign help. However, mastering nuclear technology can provide another means of protection: one that does not rely on another foreign nation. Mastering the nuclear puzzle means Iran could join the small club of nuclear weapons states: when it wants to.

NUCLEAR POWER, NUCLEAR WEAPONS OR BOTH?

Any assessment of the intentions of the IRI is necessarily speculative given the closed nature of the regime. With that in mind, a review of the literature from 1979 to the present yields three general trends for the reasons behind Tehran's nuclear pursuits; demand for energy, pursuit of great power status, and response to perceived regional threats.

The IRI consistently contends their nuclear program is solely for peaceful purposes. Bowen and Kidd in their *International Affairs* article "The Iranian Nuclear Challenge" illustrated the official Iranian position of pursuing a nuclear program to meet energy demands.[52] Citing an official Iranian document submitted to the House of Commons Foreign Affairs Committee, they list four reasons for the IRI's pursuit of nuclear power, the first being Tehran will become a net importer of crude oil if Iran continues to consume energy in the present form of fossil fuels. Secondly, increasing use of domestic fossil fuel will have a significant impact on Iran's earnings from the export of oil and natural gas. Third, fossil fuels provide greater value when used in petrochemical industries rather than power generation. Fourth, increased reliance on fossil fuels has a significant environmental impact. Indeed, Iran's energy needs are rising faster than the ability to meet them and will continue to do so over the next 15 years based on projected demand.[53] The IRI's Supreme Leader Ayatollah Ali Khamenei reinforced this official position in an August 20, 2005 speech where Khamenei stated, "For us, the nuclear issue is a scientific-economic issue. If we complete the course we have quite successfully taken so far, it would be a

---

[52] Bowen, Wyn Q. and Kidd, Joanna. "The Iranian Nuclear Challenge." International Affairs 80, 2 (2004), p. 258

[53] de Bellaigue, Christopher. "Iran" *Foreign Policy*, May/June 2005. Washington, D.C.: Carnegie Endowment for International Peace, 2005. p. 19.

scientific achievement for the country…We do not want to deplete our non-renewable energy resources and want to keep them for the next generations."[54]   To that end, the IRI and Russia agreed in 2002 to complete the $840 million reactor at Bushehr in addition to plans for up to five additional reactors for a possible $10 billion over the next decade.[55]

The second trend with respect to Iranian policy suggests the IRI is striving for great power status, or at least, to counter efforts by the United States to isolate it.[56]   Tehran is concerned about American efforts to undermine the IRI's economy and diplomatic activity as well as threats from Israel to attack the IRI nuclear infrastructure.[57]   Additionally, in a 1995 *Survival* article "Does Iran Want Nuclear Weapons?" Shahram Chubin argues the IRI sees itself as victimized and encircled, hence with both ambition and security concerns in the region.   This mix of ambition and security concerns is a position similar to that of the shah in 1814, victimized in defeat by the Russians, but harboring ambitions on regaining lost ground.

Chubin also contends the Islamic Republic believes it has a mission that goes beyond national interests to include the entire Muslim world which it views as mistreated by the current international system.[58]   With the knowledge, that India and Pakistan both have nuclear weapons; a nuclear program is a matter of nationalism.[59]   The Iranians may want nuclear technology to show they are an advanced, fully developed nation and to show the world that "Shiite Iran is the greatest society in Southwest Asia."[60] To be the greatest society in Southwest Asia, regain some of the glory of the Persian empires of the past, and protect the revolution, the IRI requires self-

---

[54] "Iran Stands like a Mountain in Pursuing its Nuclear Rights: Leader," *Tehran Times*, 20 August 2005. www.tehrantimes.com, accessed 21 Aug 05

[55] Baker, Peter. "Putin's Concessions to U.S. are Limited the Bottom Line, Russia Unyielding on Iran Nuclear Project," *The Washington Post*, 16 August 2002.

[56] de Bellaigue, p. 19

[57] Eisenstadt, Michael. "Living with a Nuclear Iran?" *Survival*, Autumn, 1999. London: International Institute for Strategic Studies, p. 127.

[58] Chubin, Shahram. "Does Iran Want Nuclear Weapons?" *Survival*, Spring, 1995. London: International Institute for Strategic Studies, p. 101.

[59] Bowen and Kidd, p. 265

[60] Perkovich, George. "For Tehran, Nuclear Program is a Matter of National Pride." *Yale Global*, 21 March 2005. Washington, D.C.: Carnegie Endowment for International Peace, 2005.

sufficiency and independence.[61] This may explain, in part, the natural gas and oil agreement signed with China in 2004 worth up to $70 billion over the next 30 years as well as a $2 billion agreement with Japan to develop the Azadegan oilfield in southwestern Iran.[62]

A successful nuclear program would address all of these concerns by improving the standing of the regime throughout Iran and the Muslim world, projecting the image of an advanced society throughout the region and relieving some of the perceived victimization by gaining a seat at the table with the other nuclear powers. At the same time, the IRI would be able to attempt to intimidate the Arab Gulf States and undermine their confidence in American security guarantees in an effort to reduce the US military presence in the Gulf.

The third trend in the IRI's nuclear program is a response to perceived threats. Iran bridges the gap between the Middle Eastern and Central Asian regions, neither of which is particularly stable. The perceived threat is direct attack by either Israel or the United States.[63] This perception is reinforced by the current deployment of US forces in Iraq and Afghanistan along with a continued US naval presence in the Persian Gulf, effectively encircling Iran.[64] The IRI may be taking lessons from the US response to its fellow members of the "axis of evil", Iraq and North Korea. North Korea declared a nuclear capability and the US pursued six party talks; Iraq did not have such a capability and the US invaded. This line of thinking is rather simplistic but fielding a nuclear weapon will provide the IRI with the capability to threaten US allies Israel, Turkey, Egypt, Jordan, or Saudi Arabia in order to gain advantage over the US in the event of

---

[61] Bowen and Kidd, p. 265

[62] de Bellaigue, Christopher. "Iran" *Foreign Policy*, May/June 2005. Washington, D.C.: Carnegie Endowment for International Peace, 2005. p. 19. AFP. "Japan to Develop Iran Oilfield." *AlJazeera.net*, www.english.aljazeera.net, accessed 15 February 2006.

[63] Jones, Peter. "Iran's Threat Perceptions and Arms Control Policies." *The Nonproliferation Review*, Fall 1998, p. 44. Venter, Al J. *Iran's Nuclear Option, Tehran's Quest for the Atom Bomb.* Havertown: Casemate Publishers, 2005, p. 121.

[64] Bowen and Kidd, p. 264.

conflict. Further, such a capability may deter retaliation for attempts to disrupt oil shipments from the Gulf or close the Strait of Hormuz.[65]

What do these trends tell us about Tehran's motives? Viewing Iranian behavior from the Western theoretical perspectives of realism, liberalism, and idealism provides a means of gaining insight into the intentions of the IRI.

A WESTERN PERSPECTIVE

The realist perspective of international relations is a pessimistic one. While realists believe a peaceful world is desirable there is no escaping the competition between states for power. To that end, the realist theory of international relations is based on three core beliefs. First, nation-states are the principle actors in international politics. Second, realists believe the primary influence on nation-states is the external environment rather than by the internal characteristics of the state. Third, a distinction between "good" and "bad" states is not as important as the competition between states for power and influence in their own self-interest.[66]

From the realist perspective, Iran has enemies on three of its borders and is therefore in an intense competition for power and influence in the region. The United States, one of its two primary enemies, is present to the east, west, and south. Given the threat, the IRI might attempt to bolster its military power by pursuing a nuclear option while using diplomacy to frustrate efforts on the part of the European Union and the US to prevent it. A stronger Iranian military increases the nation's influence in the region, improves the security of the regime by deterring attacks from regional or global rivals (Israel and America in particular) and moves the IRI toward regional hegemony. As a nuclear power, the IRI will have a seat in the nuclear club and be dominant nation in the region militarily. Notably, a realist perspective would not support the

---

[65] Eisenstadt, p. 126.
[66] Mearsheimer, John J. *The Tragedy of Great Power Politics.* New York: W. W. Norton and Company, 2001, pp. 17-22.

Iranian government's official position for its nuclear program, an improved economy. However, a second Western perspective, liberalism, does.

The liberalism theory of international relations also has three core beliefs. First, nation states are the main actors in international politics. Second, liberals believe the internal characteristics of states vary and these characteristics have significant effect on the behavior of the state. Additionally, many liberal theorists contend some governmental arrangements are inherently better than others (democracy vs., dictatorships for example). Therefore, "good" states have superior governmental arrangements and work to maintain the peace while "bad" states tend to use force. Increasing the number of "good" states helps to maintain the peace. Third, liberals believe that estimations about military power are not that important when explaining the behavior of states. Instead, political and economic power is more important. Economic interdependence, the spread of democracy and international institutions to enhance cooperation between states are all parts of the liberalism theory.[67]

From the liberalism perspective, Iran is a conundrum. Iran's Islamic Theocracy places it a "bad" state category. On the other hand, the IRI is a signatory to the Nuclear Non-Proliferation Treaty (NPT) simply demanding its rights under the treaty to the nuclear fuel cycle to generate electricity thereby freeing up domestic oil and natural gas for the international market and increasing the degree economic interdependence of Iran in the global economy. At the same time, the idea that democracy will spread across the region does not take into account 2500 years of Persian history. In fact, the semi-authoritarian, anti-Western Islamic theocracy of the IRI is a democracy in name only. The third perspective of international relations theory, idealism, provides some insight to the relationship between the theocracy and the international community.

Idealism contends international relations develop through persuasive ideas, collective values, culture and identities. In contrast to the previous two theories, states are not key actors.

---

[67] Mearsheimer, pp. 15-16.

Instead, the primary players are nongovernmental organizations, promoters of ideas, and transnational activist networks. The main instruments of the theory are ideas and values. Since September of 2001, idealism has seen resurgence because it emphasizes the role of ideology, cultural identity and transnational networks in the behavior of actors within the international system. As such, idealists would expect the ideology of the Iranian regime to play a dominant role in its behavior.[68]

Through the perspective of idealism, the cultural and social identities put in place by the Iranian regime shape the view of other nations vis-à-vis the IRI as well as what international policies it pursues. In particular, Iran supports "transnational activist networks" such as Hamas, Islamic Jihad, and most importantly Hezbollah. Through these organizations, Tehran has exported the ideals of the 1979 revolution for decades. According to the US State Department's 2003 *Patterns of Global Terrorism* Iran remained the most active state sponsor of terrorism.[69] Efforts to develop nuclear capabilities, both for the generation of electricity and weapons, serves to protect promote the ideas, culture and social identity of the 1979 revolution.

By themselves, none of these Western perspectives describes Tehran's intentions behind the pursuit of a nuclear program. However, when used as a kaleidoscope, these lenses of international relations provide potential insight into the IRI's view of the world. Building a series of nuclear reactors over the next decade with the help of Russia and within NPT guidelines will enable the IRI to benefit from the demand for fossil fuels by the growing economies of the world. Additionally, it is apparent the IRI will not operate like a Western democracy when dealing with other nations and can, if provoked, pose a threat to these democracies through its continuing ideological and financial support of terrorism through Hamas, Islamic Jihad, and Hezbollah. Finally, the nuclear pursuits of the IRI protect the regime and expand its influence in the region,

---

[68] Snyder, Jack. "One World, Rival Theories." *Foreign Policy*, November/December 2004. Washington, D.C.: Carnegie Institute for International Peace, 2004, pp. 59-60.
[69] *Patterns of Global Terrorism 2003*. Washington, D.C.: United States Department of State, April 2004, p. 86.

particularly if weapons are fielded. To gain a seat in the nuclear club, and the influence that comes with such a seat, the IRI will have to both produce and detonate a weapon. Rather than comparing the outcomes of Iraq and North Korea, a more effective comparison might be that of India and North Korea. India detonated a nuclear weapon in a very dangerous part of the world at a very delicate time, weathered the diplomatic storm, and entered the nuclear club. In contrast, North Korea has not detonated a weapon, resorted to international blackmail, and become more isolated than ever. To gain the maximum power and regional influence from a nuclear program, the IRI will have to field and detonate a weapon.

The desire to field a nuclear weapon to counter perceived threats, attain regional power status, and generate electricity to improve the local economy is one thing. Actually fielding a weapon is quite another. Reviewing the IRI's capabilities with respect to the technologies required to field a nuclear weapon provides some insight into the status and prospects of Iran's nuclear program. In particular, is it too late to prevent the IRI from being able to field a nuclear weapon at a time of its choosing?

IS THE GENIE ALREADY OUT OF THE BOTTLE?

The technical capability needed for the Iranian government to produce a nuclear weapon at a time of their choosing falls into three general categories; availability of uranium or plutonium (or control of the nuclear fuel cycle), trained personnel, and a bomb design. By February of 2006, with 20 years of effort behind it, Tehran has what it needs to produce a weapon. While additional assistance from other countries or the black market might speed up the timeline, preventing Iran from being able to field a nuclear weapon if it wants to is no longer realistic. The genie is already out of the bottle.

TICKLE THE TAIL OF THE DRAGON OR SURF THE WEB?

In the information age, a bomb design may be the easiest capability to acquire, quite a change from 1942 when scientists arriving at Los Alamos received a short primer on what was known about building a nuclear weapon.[70] In an effort to study the amount of material needed for a nuclear weapon the Los Alamos scientists would pull pieces of metal through rings of the same material. It was called the Dragon experiment and was dangerous enough that it was said to be like "tickling the tail of a sleeping dragon."[71] Today such a risky approach is no longer necessary.

In November 2005, the Director General of the IAEA reported to the organization's Board of Governors that inspectors had found documents in Iran related to a 1987 offer made by a "foreign intermediary" that address the "procedural requirements for…the casting and machining of enriched, natural and depleted uranium metal into hemispherical forms."[72] *AFP*, in a related article, quoted Gary Samore, a former Clinton administration official as saying, "There is no other purpose for manufacturing highly enriched uranium in hemispheres except for nuclear weapons."[73] A similar article in the *New York Times*, also in November 2005, reported on the contents of a stolen Iranian laptop computer. According to the *Times*, the computer contained studies on design features of a nuclear device to include a sphere of detonators for conventional explosives. The credibility of the laptop information is a matter of debate in the international community according to the *Times*. [74] Further, it is widely believed the smuggling network of Pakistani scientist A.Q. Khan provided a weapon design, along with centrifuge technology, to Libya.[75] Since Dr. Khan has admitted to supplying information to both Iran and Libya, Iran may have received a bomb design as part of the purchase.

---

[70] Serber, Robert. *The Los Alamos Primer. The First Lectures on How to Build an Atomic Bomb.* Berkeley: University of California Press, 1992.

[71] Ibid, a photo of the mechanism is included in the photograph section of the book.

[72] *Implementation of the NPT Safeguards Agreement in the Islamic Republic of Iran.* International Atomic Energy Agency, 18 November 2005.

[73] AFP. "Iran May Have Handed Over Nuclear Core Plan by Accident." 20 November 2005. *Khaleej Times Online*, www.khaleejtimes.com, accessed 16 February 2006.

[74] Broad, William J. and Sanger, David E. "The Laptop. Relying on Computer, U.S. seeks to Prove Iran's Nuclear Aims." *The New York Times*. 13 November 2005.

[75] Squassoni, Sharon A. *Weapons of Mass Destruction: Trade between North Korea and Pakistan.* Washington, D.C.: Congressional Research Service, 11 March 2004, p. 11.

However, blueprints from the Khan network are not necessarily required to produce a weapon. A great deal of general information on old weapon designs is available using the internet and a good library. Indeed, the *Progressive* magazine published the schematics of a thermonuclear weapon in 1979 after a long court battle with the Department of Energy.[76] The basics of even simpler weapon designs are also available on the internet.[77] Therefore, an important question is what kind of weapon Tehran would attempt to produce, one that fits on a Shahab-3 ballistic missile or one that fits in a shipping container, or both? Either way, general bomb design information must couple with technical expertise to field a weapon. This expertise has been available to Tehran through its relations with Russia, China, and Pakistan.

LEARNING THE ROPES

Ironically, the beginnings of Iran's technical knowledge in the nuclear arena began with the United States during the reign of Mohammand Reza Shah Pahlavi. The Iranian nuclear power program began in the mid 1950s and moved slowly through the late 1960s. During this time, the US supplied Iran with a research reactor that is still in operation today at the Tehran Nuclear Research Center. Additionally, young Iranian scientists went to the US and Europe to study nuclear physics and engineering. In the 1970s, Iran had a well-trained group of scientists and made plans to build more than 20 nuclear power plants as well as conducting initial research into military applications.[78] However, these plans had just begun when the 1979 revolution brought the program to a halt. The leaders of the new Islamic Republic stopped construction on two West German supplied reactors at Bushehr. In the mid-1980s, the IRI revived its nuclear program, partly in response to Iraqi chemical weapon attacks in the Iraq – Iran war. Since the majority of the scientists previously trained had left Iran during the revolution, the IRI turned to new partners

---

[76] Morland, Howard. "The H-bomb Secret, to Know How is to Ask Why." *The Progressive.* November 1979, p. 3-12.
[77] See for example www.nuclearweaponarchive.org.
[78] Zahedi, Ardeshir. "Iran's Nuclear Ambitions." *Wall Street Journal*, 25 June 2004.

in China and Pakistan while also offering inducements for expatriates to return to Iran. Iranian scientists began training in both China and Pakistan in 1987.[79] More recently, Iran allegedly received the designs for Pakistani P1 and P2 gas centrifuges used in the enrichment of uranium from the Khan network.[80] Iranian scientists have traveled to Pakistan as part of the agreements with the Khan network. Finally, Russia has provided training in the operation of the light water reactors at Bushehr as part of the agreements to complete the reactors. While sending students to Russia, the IRI has also attempted to recruit former Russian nuclear scientists.[81] This sort of training combined with the ability to control the nuclear fuel cycle would provide Tehran the ability to run nuclear power plants, field a nuclear weapon, or both. All that remains is the acquisition of uranium or plutonium through theft, smuggling, or an indigenous nuclear fuel cycle.

WEAPONS GRADE MATERIAL – THE RIGHT STUFF

The former Soviet Union states are the biggest potential source of uranium or plutonium. The material can come in the form of fuel rods from a reactor, highly enriched uranium from a facility that was once part of the Soviet nuclear weapons complex, or actual bomb components. For example, in 1993 the US ambassador to Kazakhstan received information on a warehouse full of nuclear material. The abandoned facility at the Ulba Metallurgy Plant was once part of the Soviet Ministry of Atomic Energy and produced highly enriched uranium for the reactors on Soviet submarines. In 1993 however, the warehouse contained 1,278 pounds of highly enriched uranium protected by a single padlock. In terms of weapons, that is enough for approximately

---

[79] Boureston, Jack and Ferguson, Charles D. "Schooling Iran's Atom Squad." *Bulletin of the Atomic Scientists*, May/June 2004 (vol. 60, no. 03), pp.31-35.
[80] Cirincione, Joseph, Wolfsthal, Jon B. and Rajkumar, Miriam. *Deadly Arsenals, Nuclear, Biological, and Chemical Threats*, 2nd Ed. Washington, D.C.: Carnegie Endowment for International Peace, 2005.
[81] Boureston and Ferguson, pp. 31-35.

twenty crude bombs. [82] In such an environment, it is unlikely anyone can accurately predict the amount of highly enriched uranium produced in the former Soviet states, much less account for all of it. This type of accounting problem also exists with the 22,000 tactical nuclear weapons in the Soviet arsenal at the end of the Cold War. In the fall of 1991, the Russian government set about moving these weapons from field units and securing them in Russia. In May 1992, the Russian government declared the project completed. The difficulty of moving 22,000 nuclear weapons in such a short time without losing any is significant.[83] Even a 99 percent success rate would leave 220 weapons missing. Inflation in Russia at the time was 2,000 percent and the military personnel responsible for the weapons were not necessarily paid. Graham Allison in his book *Nuclear Terrorism* sums up the problem this way, "In light of these realities, is it conceivable that 22,000 nuclear weapons…were recovered without a single loss?"[84]

While theft and smuggling are viable routes for Tehran to pursue, a longer-term solution to the acquisition of uranium or plutonium for either reactor fuel rod production or a weapon is to develop an indigenous nuclear fuel cycle. The pursuit of such a capability lies at the heart of the negotiations between Iran, the European Union and the IAEA from 2003 to the present.

The nuclear fuel cycle; from mining and milling uranium to fissile material (the material for bombs) production is, "By far the most costly, complicated, and observable part of building nuclear weapons…"[85] Indeed, Iran has been pursuing a complete fuel cycle since 1985 when Atomic Energy Organization of Iran (AEOI) officials discovered a large uranium deposit in the Saghand region of the Yazd province. A diagram of the basics of the fuel cycle is in figure 2. While it is unclear how much progress Iran has really made toward an indigenous fuel cycle

---

[82] Allison, Graham. *Nuclear Terrorism, the Ultimate Preventable Catastrophe.* New York: Owl Books, Henry Holt and Company, 2005, p. 64.
[83] Ibid, p. 70.
[84] Ibid.
[85] Cirincione et al, p. 45.

capability, Tehran announced it intended to close its nuclear fuel cycle and reiterated that position in November 2005.[86]

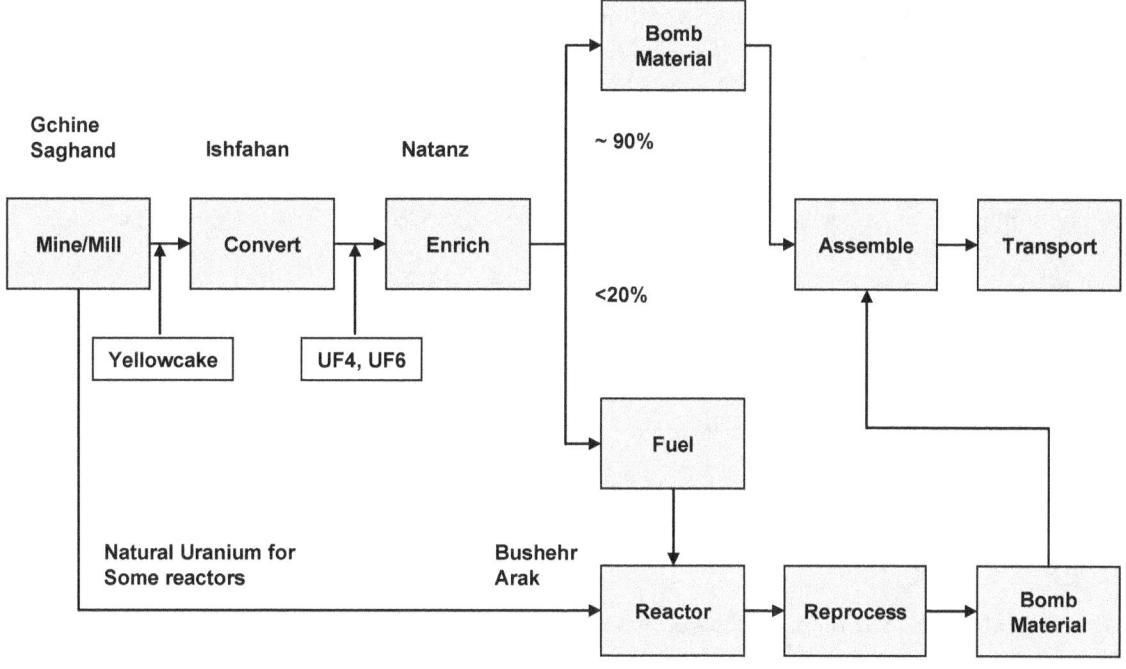

Figure 2: Nuclear Fuel Cycle

Beginning with uranium mining and milling, Iran currently has at least two uranium mines, one at Saghand and one in Gchine. Mills are located near the mines. The raw uranium ore from the ground is subjected to a mechanical and chemical milling process to produce yellowcake.[87] Andrew Koch and Jeanette Wolf in a 1997 article for *The Nonproliferation Review* illustrate the external assistance received by Iran after internal efforts to mine and mill the uranium failed; China assisted with further exploration, Russia with mining and milling the uranium ore.[88]

The next step in the fuel cycle is the conversion of the yellowcake into uranium tetrafluoride (UF4) and then to uranium hexafluoride (UF6). Tehran converts uranium in a facility

---

[86] Karimi, Nasser. "Iran Seeks Nuclear Fuel Guarantee," *Philadelphia Inquirer*, 28 November 2005.

[87] Koch, Andrew and Wolf, Jeanette. "Iran's Nuclear Procurement Program: How Close to the Bomb?" *The Nonproliferation Review*, Fall 1997, p. 124. Also, see Allison, p. 99.

[88] Ibid, pp. 123-124.

at Isfahan.[89] Iran informed the IAEA in 1996 of plans to build a uranium conversion facility at

Isfahan. Once again, China provided the plans along with technical assistance for the facility.[90]

At the time, the announcement raised questions about Iran's intent to enrich uranium. Since

Russia will supply the fuel for the reactors at Bushehr, there was no reason for Iran to produce

uranium hexafluoride. Uranium hexafluoride is the feedstock for a gas centrifuge plant to enrich

uranium in preparation for use as reactor fuel or in a nuclear weapon. The most controversial,

and most critical, part of the fuel cycle is the enrichment of uranium.

In August of 2002, the National Council of Resistance to Iran (an Iranian opposition

group) released information suggesting Tehran was developing a uranium enrichment facility.

Tehran admitted in February 2003 the existence of the facility as well as having pursued an

enrichment capability since 1985. An IAEA inspection yielded a pilot enrichment plant at Natanz

operating 160 gas centrifuges while workers were assembling 1,000 more.[91]

The gas centrifuges in question appear to be of Pakistani origin, most likely acquired the

Khan network. The general concept of operation for a gas centrifuge plant is to arrange the

centrifuges into one or more cascades (a group of centrifuges) and feed uranium hexafluoride into

the plant recovering both enriched uranium and depleted uranium. Initially the uranium

hexafluoride fed into the cascade generally contains 0.5-0.7% uranium-235 (U-235). Anything

over 20% U-235 is considered "highly enriched" by international standards, but an enrichment

level of about 90% is generally desired for use in a weapon.[92] Light water reactors like the one at

Bushehr require enrichment levels of 2-3% U-235.[93] The amount of time required for the

---

[89] Ibid, p. 124.

[90] Hibbs, Mark. "Iran Told IAEA it Will Build Chinese UF6 Plant at Isfahan," *NuclearFuel*, 16 December 1996, p. 1.

[91] Albright, David. "Appendix B, Iran's Nuclear Program: Status, Risks, and Prospects," Reassessing the Implications of a Nuclear-Armed Iran (Judith Yaphe and Charles Lutes). Washington, D.C.: Institute for National Strategic Studies, National Defense University, 2005, pp. 67-68.

[92] *In Depth, Nuclear Fuel Cycle*. BBC News, UK Edition. http://news.bbc.co.uk/2/hi/in_depth/world/2003/nuclear_fuel_cycle/mining/default.stm, accessed 28 October 2005.

[93] Ibid.

enrichment plant to produce enough material for either reactor fuel or a bomb depends on many variables such as size and efficiency of the centrifuges, number of centrifuges in a cascade, number of cascades and batch recycling. Batch recycling involves taking the enriched uranium hexafluoride from the centrifuge plant and using it as the feedstock for another run. To illustrate, if the U-235 level went from 0.5% to 1.5%, utilizing the 1.5% "batch" as the feedstock is an example of batch recycling. Whether or not batch recycling is part of the process, and how many times it is used, are two more variables in how long it takes an enrichment plant to produce the required amount of U-235.

Referring again to figure 2, if the enrichment plant at Natanz produces 90% highly enriched uranium, Tehran could go straight to bomb production using designs from the black market or elsewhere once the fluoride is removed through cooling and a chemical process. On the other hand, if the enriched uranium is for a reactor, the fluoride is removed and the resulting uranium becomes the fuel rods necessary for the reactor. Periodically, the spent fuel rods go through a reprocessing facility after removal from the reactor. Reprocessing is also a chemical process to separate usable fuel from nuclear waste and plutonium.[94] Through reprocessing, the IRI could produce enough plutonium for a weapon. As of December 2005, Iran does not have a declared reprocessing facility.

The existence of a uranium enrichment capability in Iran for supplying fuel to a nuclear reactor is suspect since Russia will supply the fuel for Iran's only reactor (still unfinished) at Bushehr.[95] The agreement would also preclude the need for a reprocessing facility. Albright calls the enrichment effort "highly dubious" and adds that in 1985 Germany had already suspended work on the Bushehr reactor. For ten years until Russia agreed to complete the Bushehr reactor, Iran continued to pursue uranium enrichment. Finally, Albright sums up the

---

[94] Ibid.

[95] Busch, Nathan. *No End in Sight, the Continuing Menace of Nuclear Proliferation.* Lexington: The University Press of Kentucky, 2004.

concerns of many vis-à-vis Iran's nuclear weapons program as "the timing, scope, and long secrecy of the program have led many nations to conclude that Iran either had or has one."[96] Given that Iran has been working on the enrichment of uranium for 18 years, how soon could Tehran have enough highly enriched uranium for a nuclear weapon?

Albright in *McNair Paper 69*, based on the Natanz plant, and with information from IAEA reports estimates the earliest date Iran could field a weapon as early 2007.[97] The longer the IRI does not enrich uranium as a part of the negotiations, the longer it will take to produce the fissile material required for a weapon.

In December 2005, *Aljazeera* quoted Meir Dagan, the head of the Israeli Mossad, in a statement before Israeli members of parliament that Iran was two years away from having a nuclear weapon.[98] However, the Israeli estimate in December of 2005 was a moving target. On December 27, the *Jerusalem Post* quoted Dagan as reporting Iran was six months away from "technological independence."[99] In the same article, the *Post* quoted the IDF Chief of Staff, Lt. Gen Dan Halutz, from a December 13 statement as saying the IRI would not be able to develop a bomb before 2008.[100]

Of course, all the assessments of the status of Iran's nuclear program have one critical assumption; the IRI has revealed all of their nuclear facilities and activities. Bowen and Kidd summarize the current assessment of Iran's nuclear weapons program very effectively: "Given Tehran's active concealment of enrichment and plutonium-related activities, it is difficult to avoid the conclusion that Iran is pursuing the acquisition of nuclear weapons. Iran's contradictory

---

[96] Albright, p. 54.
[97] Ibid, p. 68.
[98] "Israel Rules Out Strike on Iran – for Now," *Aljazeera.net*, 29 December 2005. http://english.aljazerra.net, accessed 2 January 2006.
[99] Frankel, Rafael D. and Klass, Oren. "Dagan: One Nuke not Enough for Iran," Jerusalem Post, online edition, 27 December 2005. www.jpost.com, accessed 2 January 2006.
[100] Ibid.

33

claims and obfuscation throughout 2003 support this assessment and add to concerns that other facilities and activities may well remain hidden from the IAEA."[101]

WHAT TO DO?

Tehran's continued "obfuscation", resumption of uranium conversion in 2005 and "nuclear research" in January of 2006 continue to support this assessment. [102] When Tehran is able to close the nuclear fuel cycle by enriching uranium, all the technical pieces will be in place for Iran to field a nuclear weapon at a time of their choosing. The question then becomes, "How can the risks posed by a nuclear-armed Iran be managed?"

To date the reaction of the international community has centered on negotiations between the EU-3 (Britain, Germany, and France) and Iran. These negotiations stopped in August 2005 when Iran resumed uranium conversion. While the parties had returned to the table in December 2005, the talks did not produce any progress toward preventing Iran from closing the nuclear fuel cycle and the IAEA reported the Iranian dossier to the United Nations Security Council in February 2006. In general the debates in open literature about what should be done center around either some sort of grand bargain between Iran and the world or a military strike on Iran's nuclear infrastructure.

The military analogy most often used is the Israeli raid on the Iraqi reactor at Osirak in June 1981. Iraq signed the non-proliferation treaty in 1969 and purchased a reactor from France in 1975. International concern over the Iraqi program grew in September 1980, during the early part of the Iran-Iraq war, when the Iraq issued the statement "The Iranian people should not fear the Iraqi nuclear reactor, which is not intended to be used against Iran, but against the Zionist entity."[103] Faced with a direct and explicit threat, Israel elected not to trust diplomatic efforts with

---

[101] Bowen and Kidd, p. 261
[102] Associated Press. "Iran to Resume Nuke Program in Face of Referral to UN Security Council," 4 February 2006. www.foxnews.com, accessed 4 February 2005
[103] Grant, Rebecca. "Osirak and Beyond," *AIR FORCE Magazine*, August 2002, p. 75

France to curtail the Iraqi program and attacked in June of 1981. Destruction of the reactor by a strike package of Israeli F-15s and F-16s took less than two minutes once they reached the reactor.[104]

However, this type of raid would be significantly more complicated with Iran's infrastructure. First, there are at least seven widely dispersed sites in Iran, not one.[105] More troubling are the number of sites in existence about which we do not know. Since Iran kept the nuclear program a secret for 18 years, and then only admitted to the existence of nuclear facilities after a resistance group leaked the information, an attacker must assume there are more facilities. Second, Iran is much larger than Iraq and much farther away from Israel than Osirak. While striking these sites is certainly possible, given the uncertainty in the number and location of the facilities (of how many was the international community aware before August 2002?) such a strike may only have a very low probability of shutting down the Iranian nuclear program and brings with it any number of consequences. That said, developing such a plan is both prudent and necessary.

The other general option is the so-called grand bargain. This approach requires the West to use economic incentives to force the Iranian government into a decision between economic well-being and nuclear weapons. Such incentives may include support for entry into the World Trade Organization, lifting sanctions, or increasing investment.[106] Iran would give up its nuclear program (or dramatically curtail it) in return for the economic package. Finally, Iran would be subject to the threat of force in the event Tehran returned to its nuclear program. Such a bargain requires a degree of unity among the Western nations that does not currently exist. Additionally, it is not clear Iran is concerned about the threat of force. As Azadeh Moaveni wrote in a December 2004 issue of Al-Ahram Weekly, "With little sign of a shift in Washington, Iranian

---

[104] Ibid, p. 75.
[105] Cirincione et al, p. 294.
[106] Pollack, Kenneth and Takeyh, Ray. "Taking on Tehran," Foreign Affairs, March/April 2005. New York: Council on Foreign Relations, 2005.

officials are relaxing in their positions, comfortable with a horizon of interim deals they can neuter through nit-picking."[107] Finally, the IRI's acceptance of this grand bargain would not be consistent with its efforts to protect the regime, expand its influence in the region, and gain a seat in the nuclear club.

Since neither the preventive strike nor the grand bargain appears very attractive, another approach would be useful. To develop such an approach a methodology is needed that synthesizes the Iranian historical pattern of balancing one foreign power with another while simultaneously seeking to limit foreign influence with the Western perspectives of international politics and the technical realities of Iran's nuclear program. One such approach, which has its roots in the region, is systemic operational design.

SYSTEMIC OPERATIONAL DESIGN

BACKGROUND

Systemic Operational Design (SOD) conceptually originated in the mid-1990s in the Israeli Defense Force (IDF). Originating at the Operational Theory Research Institute, SOD was an extensive conceptual update to the paradigm of operational art within the IDF. Primarily, SOD is an application of systems theory to operational art. SOD employs a systems approach that focuses on the relationships between the entities within a system to translate strategic direction and policy into an operational design. A cycle of design, plan, act and learn is accomplished through seven discourses leading to a holistic view of an operation.[108]

SOD is unique in many ways, one of which is that it does not assume a strategic directive is final or complete. Instead, the initial approach is to ask, "How should I think about the

---

[107] Moaveni, Azadeh. "Storm in a Teacup," Al–Ahram Weekly, Issue 721, 16-22 December 2004. http://weekly.ahram.org.eg/2004/721/re6.htm, accessed 16 February 2006.
[108] Sorrells, William, Downing, Glen R., Blakesley, Paul J., Pendhall, David W., Walk, Jason K. and Wallwork, Richard D. *Systemic Operational Design: An Introduction.* Unpublished monograph. School of Advanced Military Studies, US Army Command and General Staff College, AY 04-05.

problem" rather than "what is the problem." Another unique factor is that SOD does not attempt to be predictive but seeks to understand the relationships between entities within a system. As such SOD requires the designer (the US military might say "planner" or "strategist") to first define the system under study. Throughout the design, plan, act cycle the designer is continually learning about the system and its behavior.

Given the complex, adaptive, and emergent behavior of systems leading to an enormous number of permutations SOD does not attempt to plan a campaign from beginning to a specific end state. Instead, SOD accounts for the changes in system behavior through an iterative approach. The vehicle for changing the system behavior is the strategic raid.[109] In this context, a strategic raid does not necessarily fall into the current doctrinal definition of a raid.[110]

THE STRATEGIC RAID

From a U.S. military perspective the term "strategic raid" is potentially misleading since it combines an action (the raid) with a level of war or political result. An alternative would be to use just the term "raid" based on the Merriam-Webster Online definition; "1a. A hostile or predatory incursion, b. a surprise attack by a small force."[111] Another alternative is to use the term "special operation."

A number of definitions on "special operation" are available. Hoffman in a 1985 RAND study defined a "commando raid" as "small-scale attacks carried out by small groups behind enemy lines, using stealth and rapid mobility to achieve their missions."[112] Another definition of "special operation" from Lutwak et al is "self-contained acts of war mounted by self-sufficient forces operating within hostile territory." Lutwak et al further state "there is no absolute

---

[109] Sorrells et al, p. 20.

[110] Joint Publication 1-02. *Department of Defense Dictionary of Military and Associated Terms*, 12 April 2001 as amended through 31 August 2005. A "Raid" is defined as "an operation, usually small scale, involving a swift penetration of hostile territory to secure information, confuse the enemy, or to destroy installations. It ends with a planned withdrawal upon completion of the assigned mission."

[111] http://www.m-w.com/dictionary/raid, accessed 13 March 2006.

[112] Hoffman, Bruce. *Commando Raids: 1946-1983*. Santa Monica: RAND, 1985, p. 2.

distinction between special operations and raiding actions mounted by regular-type forces, and especially elite forces of various kinds." Moreover, Lutwak et al list six planning principles for successful operations. Among these is "surprise is paramount to all else." [113] Within SOD, the purpose of a strategic raid is to affect change within the system and provide an opportunity to learn more about the system in order to progress toward a strategic aim. To affect the rival system does not necessarily require a presence in hostile territory, however. Additionally, there is no requirement for the military to execute a raid (freezing bank accounts, for example). Therefore, for the purpose of this monograph, the definition of a strategic raid is, "a self-contained act executed by self-sufficient elements within the context of the operational design."

The operational design process consists of seven discourses, shown in figure 3, steering the designer from the broad and abstract to the narrow and concrete in a fluid and iterative process toward a final design or operational plan. The first six frames will be discussed in detail shortly, but a note regarding the final frame, forms of function, is necessary. The eventual form an action takes on is the subject of the forms of function frame. In the IDF methodology, the form of function frame is the translation of the design into a tactical plan for execution. Here the culture difference between the IDF and the US military requires an adjustment to the methodology. In the US military, this is the realm of the mission planning cell, mission commander, or flight lead. However, from an interagency view, the form of an action is still relevant to the design and the concept of a strategic raid to change the rival system is equally valid. This monograph will use the first six of the seven discourses to develop an understanding of the relationships in a system involving a nuclear-armed Iran within the context of the region and propose a direction for action to disrupt the adversary as system.

---

[113] Lutwak, Edward, Canby, Steven and Thomas, David. *A Systematic Review of "Commando" (Special) Operations 1939-1980.* Potomac: C&L Associates, 1982, p. I-1, I-34.

Photo Removed Due to Copyright Restrictions

Figure 3: Systemic Operational Design Overview[114]

A NUCLEAR-ARMED IRAN, FRAMING THE SYSTEM

This frame defines the system under study. The goal is to relate the broad context of strategic directives to the specific context of the current issue at hand. SOD recognizes the inherent system of systems nature of the world, however, the complexity involved with a truly global view is simply too great for effective action. In order to design realistic options the designer must define a subset of the global system. System framing accomplishes this by pulling together related elements to define a smaller system with respect to the issue requiring study. This smaller system is the frame, or the boundary, for further discourse.

The system frame is shown in figure 4. Around the outside, the frame is wrapped in the context of history. In the center is Iran, a country and government caught between memories of Persian glory and the realities of the modern balance of power; a position intensified by a two centuries old desire to limit foreign influence. At the same time, the government is caught between the idealism of an Islamic Theocracy and changing demographics. With this change

---

[114] Naveh, Shimon BG (res) Dr. *Questions of Operational Art, the Depth Structure of SOD.* Operational Theory Research Institute, December 2005, p. 14.

comes less revolutionary fervor but solid nationalism.[115] However, Iran is also caught between

terrorism and international norms. Support for terrorism over the years has led to isolation, not

expansion of the revolution. This isolation has put Iran between sanctions and international trade.

Oil is king, but the country's actions as a supporter of terrorism have prevented the realization of

the potential offered by a global economy.

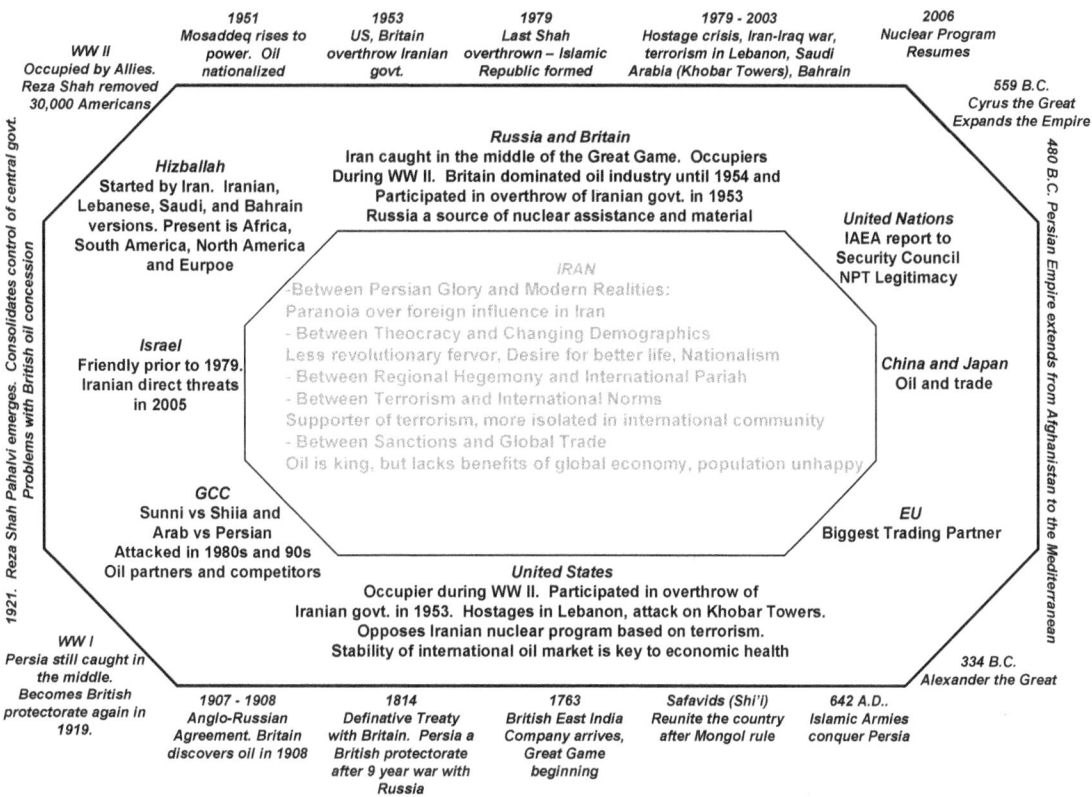

Figure 4: Nuclear-Armed Iran -- System Frame

Arrayed around Iran are various actors on both the regional and global stage. Russia and

Britain are present as always; with Britain a part of the European Union 3 (EU-3; Britain,

Germany, and France) and Russia a source for nuclear information and material as well as a

potential foil for the EU-3. The United Nations took its place in the headlines in February 2006

when the IAEA reported the Iranian nuclear dossier to the Security Council. To be sure, the

---

[115] Rubin, Michael. *The Radioactive Republic of Iran*. American Enterprise Institute for Public Policy Research, www.aei.org/publication23682, accessed 15 February 2005

40

official report from the IAEA will not be delivered until March 2006, but the UN and the IAEA must now consider the legitimacy of the NPT and its enforcement as well as the Iranian dossier when deliberations begin. One of the permanent voting members of the Security Council, China, has significant economic interests in the Iranian oil and gas industry along with Japan. China and Iran agreed to an oil and liquefied natural gas deal in 2004 that could be worth up to $70 billion over 30 years while the Japanese company Inpex agreed to a $2 billion deal to develop the Azadegan oilfield.[116] Currently, Iran's largest supplier of goods is the EU with 37 percent of Iran's total imports.[117] In that context, it is important to note France also holds a permanent voting seat on the Security Council.

Moving across the Persian Gulf, the Gulf Cooperation Council countries of Saudi Arabia, Oman, United Arab Emirates, Bahrain, Qatar, and Kuwait are faced with an uncertain security situation with respect to Iran's push for nuclear capability. While the GCC and Iran are OPEC partners, they are also competitors in the global economy. Moreover, the GCC countries are predominantly Sunni – Arab vice Shi'i – Persian. Iranian supported attacks on the some of the GCC countries in the 1980s and 1990s only add to the problem.[118] The GCC is caught in the middle between the oil demands and security guarantees of the Western economies and the cultural, political, economic and security considerations involved with a nuclear-armed Iran.

On the other side of the Middle East, but within the range of the Iranian Shahab-3 ballistic missile, lies Israel. Friendly with Iran prior to 1979, Iran threatened Israel's existence in October 2005.[119] While this is not the first time Israel has been faced with a nuclear threat, a preemptive action like the raid on Iraq's nuclear reactor is problematic for many reasons.

---

[116] de Bellaigue, p. 19. AFP, 29 December 2005, *Aljazeera.net*

[117] Perkovich, George and Manzanero, Silvia. "Iran Gets the Bomb – Then What?" *Getting Ready for a Nuclear-Armed Iran.* Sololski, Henry and Clawson, Patrick editors. Carlisle: Strategic Studies Institute.

[118] Pollack, p. 205, 209, 280-286

[119] Karimi, Nasser. Iran Leader Calls for Israel's Destruction. Associated Press, 26 October 2005.

However, faced with an existential threat, it is unreasonable to expect Israel to sit on its hands forever.

Just to the north of Israel is Lebanon, home to Hezbollah. Created in 1982 by the Islamic Revolutionary Guards following the Israeli invasion of Lebanon, Hezbollah now has an extensive international network. Representatives have been discovered in Europe, Cyprus, and the tri-border region of South America, the Philippines, Africa, Singapore and the United States.[120] The common denominator between the groups is the support of the Islamic Revolutionary Guards Corps.

The final actor in the system frame is the United States. An occupier in WW II, participant in the overthrow of the Iranian government in 1953, held hostage from 1979 – 1981, and the victim of Iranian supported attacks in the 1980s and 1990s, it might be said there is very little "good" history between the US and Iran. With respect to Iran's nuclear program the American approach has been to support the EU-3 negotiations and push for referral to the UN Security Council while also taking the position that Iran will not be allowed to have nuclear weapons (technical realities notwithstanding). The resulting tension between America and Iran presents a new set of operational level problems in the region as well as in the Global War on Terrorism. Studying the cultural, social, economic, and military elements of this rivalry is the next frame in the design methodology.

DEFINING THE RIVAL

Rival as rationale establishes the rival as a system through three efforts. The first effort is to understand the orientation of the rival by looking for patterns that suggest a reason for the rival's actions. The second is an investigation of the difference between the rival's goals, values,

---

[120] Byman, Daniel. "Should Hezbollah Be Next?" *Foreign Affairs*, Nov/Dec 2003. New York: Council on Foreign Relations, 2003.

and practices compared to the rest of the system in an effort to identify logical relationships. Third, designers characterize the rival system within the boundaries defined in system framing.

In this case, the rival frame is characterized by the tensions within the Iranian government, between the government, the people and the economy and between Iran and American interests. Iran is dominated by clerics who came to power during the revolution, but the government is not monolithic. Historically, there have always been factions such as landowners, *bazaaris*, clerics, etc. More recently, the resurgence of the hardliners over the reformers through the election of Mahmoud Ahmadinejad to the presidency demonstrates the fractious nature of the government still exists even though the inner workings are unclear. There is a demographic tension between the leading clerics and the rest of the people. With a population of approximately 68 million and a median age of 24, there is a generational gap in the country. Finally, the government has never been able to fix the economy since taking power in 1979. Some may argue such a theocracy is incapable of running a modern global economy. Whether that is true or not the fact remains Iran's economy is dependent on oil and natural gas and the infrastructure supporting the oil and gas industry is in need of modernization approximately $70 billion over the next ten years.[121]

Around the nexus of the Iranian government, people and economy are other actors and artifacts influencing the relationships within the rival system. While Iran's nuclear program is front and center now, the ramifications of the program broaden to the potential for a terrorist weapon, based on Iran's history of supporting terrorist activity. In turn, this potential is directly related to the availability of fissile material, the most difficult to attain of the three general capabilities required to field a nuclear weapon.

---

[121] Pollack and Takeyh quote this estimate from the National Iranian Oil Company. They also quote Muhammad Khazai, the deputy minister of economy and finance at the time, acknowledging the need to $20 Billion a year for five years to produce enough jobs for the country's young population.

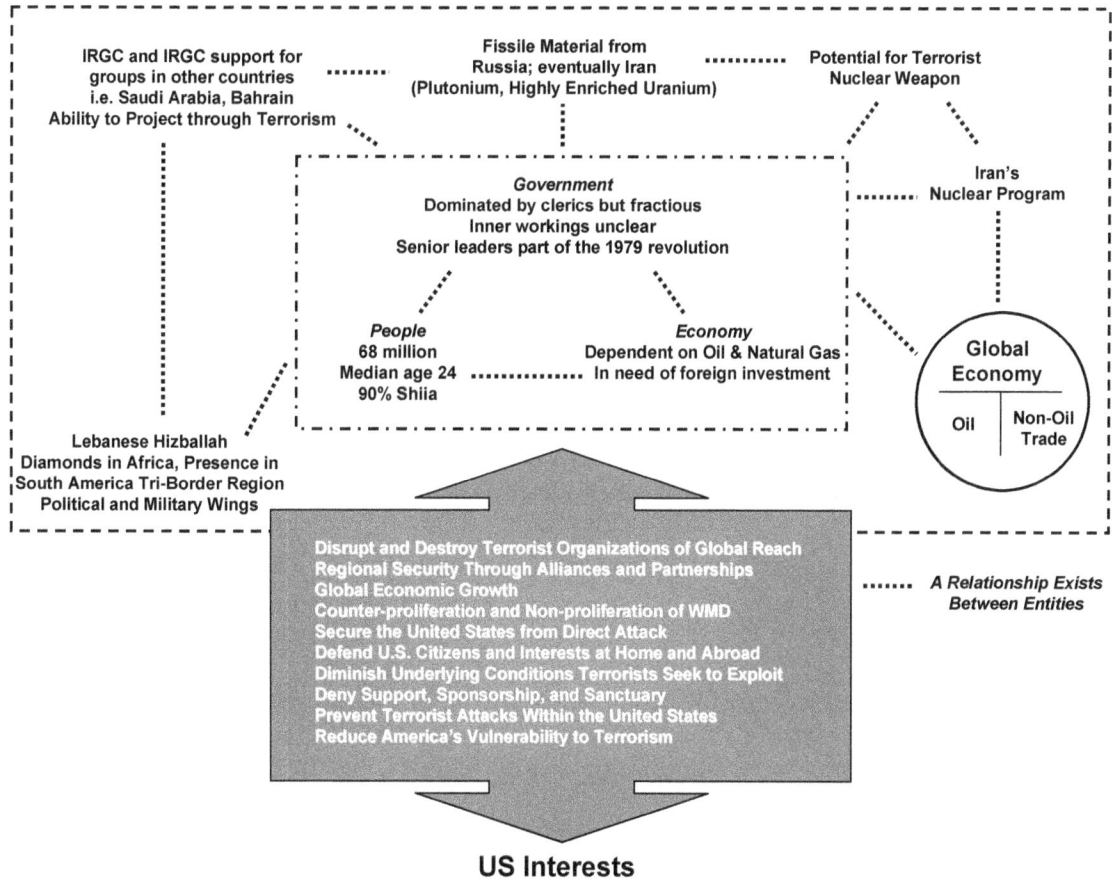

Figure 5: Nuclear-Armed Iran -- Rival Frame[122]

The Islamic Revolutionary Guards Corps (IRGC), created in May 1979 by Khomeini to

protect the revolution, is answerable only to the current Supreme Leader, Ayatollah Ali Hoseini

Khamene'i. Since 1979, it has grown to be not only a separate ministry but also the

government's trusted organization for special missions.[123] In the past, these missions have

included the creation and support of Hezbollah since 1982, support for a Saudi group to attack the

Khobar Towers in 1996 and support for a group in Bahrain in what the Bahraini government

---

[122] The US interests in figure 5 are taken from the following documents: *The National Security Strategy of the United States of America*, September 2002, *National Strategy for Combating Terrorism*, February 2003, *National Defense Strategy of the United States of America*, March 2005, *National Strategy to Combat Weapons of Mass Destruction*, December 2002, and *National Strategy for Homeland Security*, July 2002.
[123] Venter, pp. 253-270

characterized as an attempt to overthrow the government.[124] With respect to Iran's nuclear program, the IRGC controls to nuclear infrastructure. Moreover, the organization has extended its reach from Tehran to Lebanon, Africa, Europe and Cyprus. In short, the IRGC is the primary means by which Tehran projects terrorist activity around the world to further its goals and objectives.[125]

The IRGC's most famous protégé is Hezbollah in Lebanon. Started at Baalbek in the Bekaa Valley of Lebanon, Hezbollah (the Party of God) was dubbed "the A-Team of terrorists" by Deputy Secretary of State Richard Armitage. The group has both a political and a military wing; the political wing holds several seats in the Lebanese Parliament while the militant side of Hezbollah has a long record of violence. Additionally, the group has a global reach.

Iranian aid to Hezbollah estimated at as much as $100 million a year is supplemented through a variety of criminal activities in Africa, South America, and the United States. In West Africa, the group developed an extensive network during the 1980s and, since the end of the civil war in Sierra Leone in 2002, the majority of diamond buyers in the Koidu region of Sierra Leone are Lebanese. Hezbollah raises money through extortion of the Lebanese diamond merchants by threatening the merchant's families at home in Lebanon. In the Congo, however, a different approach is used. Here Hezbollah moved into the diamond trading business directly and began purchasing from local merchants and selling the better stones in the Belgian city of Antwerp. The remainder of the stones goes to markets in Dubai and Bombay. So far, Hezbollah's diamond business does not appear to be hampered by the Kimberly Process given the political strength of the merchants in Sierra Leone.[126]

In the tri-border region of South America where the borders of Paraguay, Argentina, and Brazil come together Hezbollah has participated in drug trafficking since the 1990s bringing in

---

[124] Pollack, pp. 281-282
[125] Venter, pp. 227-229
[126] MEIB Staff. "Hezbollah and the West African Diamond Trade," *Middle East Intelligence Bulletin*, June/July 2004, Vol. 6 Issue 6/7, pp. 6-8.

tens of millions of dollars.[127]   A much smaller smuggling effort was broken up in July of 2000 in

Charlotte, North Carolina. Rather than diamonds or illegal drugs, the members of the Hezbollah

cell were smuggling cigarettes. The group would buy the cigarettes in North Carolina where the

tax is only five cents a pack, sell them in Michigan where the tax is 75 cents per pack and pocket

the difference. The scheme raised as much a $2 million, some of which was passed on to a cell

in Canada to purchase military equipment and smuggle it back to Lebanon.[128] Beyond Africa and

the Americas, Hezbollah also has a significant presence in Europe. Members of the group are

believed to be located throughout Europe, the Balkans, Scandinavia, Russia, and on the

Mediterranean. All told, the global funding activities of Hezbollah bring in approximately $10

million a month.[129]

More importantly, the pattern that runs through Hezbollah's global activities, whether

finance, logistics, operations, or some combination, is the contact each cell has with senior

Hezbollah or Iranian officials.[130] The networks already in place, primarily criminal, combined

with the other common pattern of the presence of the IRGC, illustrate the potential for

relationships between Iran's nuclear program, the availability of fissile material and the ability to

project terrorism around the globe.

These patterns of global activity by the IRGC and Hezbollah along with the rhetoric out

of Tehran combine to affect the global economy through the oil market. As the rhetoric

intensifies and the prospects for successful nuclear negotiations rises and falls, so does the price

of oil. In February of 2006, the oil market at the New York Mercantile Exchange reflects a

degree of "geopolitical risk" based on the situation in Iran. In that sense, Iran has an indirect

---

[127] Ibid.

[128] Pipes, Daniel. "The Hezbollah in America," *National Review*, 28 August 2000, Vol. 52 issue 16, p. 33. Locy, Toni. "U.S. Looks at Potential Danger from Hezbollah," USA Today, 14 May 2003.

[129] Gambill, Gary C. "Dossier: Hassan Nasrallah," Middle *East Intelligence Bulletin*, Feb/Mar 2004, Vol. 6 Issue 2/3, pp. 13-22.

[130] Levitt, Matthew A. *Islamic Extremism in Europe*, FDCH Congressional Testimony, 27 April 2005, House International Relations Committee.

influence on the price of oil. As the price goes up or at least stays relatively high, the Iranian government reaps greater profits.

Finally, the relationships between the American interests of promoting a healthy global economy, regional stability, and the responsibility to protect America from attack complete the rival frame within the context of the system frame. However, the potential for a terrorist weapon presents a complex problem, particularly since the opportunity to prevent Iran from being able to field a nuclear weapon has likely already passed. To address this added complexity, an additional frame limited to the issue of a single nuclear weapon in the hands of an organization with global reach is shown in figure 6.

Photo Removed Due to Copyright Restrictions

Figure 6: Terrorist Nuke – Rival Frame[131]

---

[131] Lieggi, Stephanie and Butler, Kenley. "The Globalization of Nuclear Smuggling: Methods used by Two Pakistan-Based Networks," *NIS Export Control Observer*, May 2005. This article provides an illustration of the methods used by the A.Q. Kahn network as well as the lesser-known Karni-Kahn

Surrounding this frame are the material, logistical and other equipment requirements that influence the ability of an organization to acquire a weapon, the common theme being the need for financing to support these activities. Inside the frame the logic behind the problem begins with who has it, where the device is and where it is going, and what the intentions are of the group that possesses it (blackmail, extortion, martyrdom, etc.). Adding to the complexity is the number of ways in which the device may be obtained.

The first of these methods is by stealing one or paying another group to steal it. This relates directly to the number of former Soviet Union weapons discussed earlier. Another method is to have the weapon provided to the terrorist. As Iran moves closer to being able to field a weapon, this outcome is of greater concern. Once the IRGC controls the country's weapons, will a weapon then be provided to a proxy?

The final two acquisition methods involve shipping the uranium or plutonium to another location and putting the weapon together using either a very crude or an old design. In one case, the weapon may be built using already established facilities (in Africa for example) and transported via established networks to its target via car, shipping container, or small boat. In the other case, the device is built at the detonation site (in a warehouse for example). The material would obviously have to be shipped to the site, but this may not be as difficult as it sounds. In August 2003, ABC News successfully shipped 15 pounds of material from Jakarta, Indonesia to a storage warehouse near the Los Angeles Convention Center. The good news is the material was depleted uranium (meaning it could not be used in a bomb) the bad news is how easy it was.[132] Clearly, this approach would require several shipments and several cells to be active for an extended period. However, given the success of ABC News and the A.Q. Kahn network, it is certainly not impossible.

---

network. Besides uranium or plutonium other equipment is required to produce a nuclear weapon, some specialized and some not. "Triggered spark gaps", oscilloscopes, and machine tools are just a few examples.
    [132] Allison, pp. 104-107

The overall pattern is this frame is logistics and finance. For a group that does not have the support of a government the logistics and finance required to acquire the necessary nuclear material are extremely difficult. However, when a government is able to produce the material indigenously, and the material is in the hands of an organization with an established history of violence, the difficulty of acquisition disappears. Coupled with an ideological zeal to defend the revolution, the Iranian IRGC is just such an organization.

The rival can be summarized as a set of relationships between the tensions internal to Iran, those created by Iran's nuclear program and history of supporting terrorism through proxies, and the interests of the United States; all within the broader context of the system frame driven by the tension between the need for oil and natural gas to fuel growing economies and a resurgent hard-line government in Tehran. While the American interests include regional stability and economic growth, they are predominantly oriented toward defending against or preventing a terrorist attack on American soil. For the rival to act against these interests logistical and financial support are required along with access to nuclear material in the case of a weapon of mass destruction attack. Historically, access to the nuclear material has been the most difficult step, but this difficulty potentially dissolves when Iran is able to close the nuclear fuel cycle and enrich uranium in significant quantities. If, and when, this happens the complexity of defending against an attack grows exponentially. Militarily the problem of handling this added complexity falls partially on US Central Command since Iran is inside Central Command's area of responsibility. However, the networks of Iran and Hezbollah are global. Therefore, the problem is global. The command and logistical structures to support the operational design with respect to the system under study is the subject of command and logistics frames.

COMMAND AND LOGISTICS – STRUCTURES FOR ACTION AND LEARNING

Command as rationale examines the relationship between existing command structures and possible structures for the design at hand with respect to the system frame. This is similar to the current practice of defining the command relationships currently accomplished by military planners. If the current command structure is deemed unsuitable, the designers must examine ways to adapt the structure to support operations within the boundaries of the system frame. Designers evaluate the command structure externally to determine the impact on the operational design as well as internally to determine the impact on existing organizational structures and formations. Within the IDF, modifying the existing command structure is easier than in the US military. For the US, command as rationale is as much about discovering where the conflicts are as it is about defining the command relationships involved in an operation.

The Iranian system defined above is global in nature; therefore, the command structure will need to be global in nature. For the U.S. that means a complicated and overlapping combination of government Departments, roles, and missions. From a military standpoint, the areas of responsibility are defined in the Unified Command Plan. However, even within the Department of Defense the mission responsibilities are mixed when it comes to a nuclear-armed Iran and Iranian support for terrorism. US Central Command has the responsibility for Iran in the Middle East but Special Operations Command has the responsibility to execute global operations against terror networks and Strategic Command has the lead in combating weapons of mass destruction.[133] Closer to home, part of the Department of Homeland Security's mission is to prevent terrorist attacks within the United States and the Department of Energy is responsible for enhancing the nation's security by improving WMD detection capabilities and preventing the proliferation of WMD.[134] Certainly, the current command structure is global in nature but the overlapping responsibilities, particularly within the Department of Defense; do not point to an efficient structure.

[133] *United States Special Operations Command Mission*, US Special Operations Command, http://www.socom.mil/Docs/Command_Mission-060214.pdf, accessed 19 February 2006. *US Strategic Command SNAP SHOT*, US Strategic Command, February 2006, http://www.stratcom.mil/fact_sheets/SnapShot.doc, accessed 19 February 2006.
[134] http://www.dhs.gov/dhspublic/faq.jsp, accessed 19 February 2006. http://www.energy.gov/nationalsecurity/wmd.htm, accessed 19 February 2006.

Logistics as rationale is similar to command as rationale. Here, an examination of friendly logistics with respect to the system frame develops options within the logistics infrastructure to support the operational design. The logistics system in place to support current operations in the Middle East, counter-narcotics operations in South America, operations in Africa and operations supporting the Global War on Terrorism in general provides the infrastructure necessary for global operations within the system and rival frames. With the command a logistics structures in mind the operation is framed within the context of the system frame.

OPERATION FRAMING AND OPERATIONAL CONDITIONS

Operation framing develops a concept of operation that exploits the relationships within the rival frame to shape the system toward a set of conditions more in the designer's favor. This frame describes the form of operational maneuver within the context of the rival, command, and logistics frames and within the boundaries of the system frame. Additionally, the ending conditions for the operation, within political and strategic constraints, provide the guidelines for operational learning. Operation framing extends beyond military options and is not campaign planning nor should it be confused with phasing in a campaign plan.

Operational framing is based generally on two principles. The first is dynamic complexity where cause and effect are subtle and the full impact of various actions develops over time.[135] The second is that when one or more components of the system are acted upon, the system will self-organize and a new form or behavior will emerge. This new form or behavior cannot be directed but each action will have a consequence. The key then is to agitate the system, observe the result, and reframe to progress to the desired strategic aim (see figure 7).[136]

---

[135] Senge, Peter M. *The Fifth Discipline, the Art & Practice of the Learning Organization.* New York: Doubleday, 1990, p. 71.
[136] Pascale, Richard T., Millemann, Mark and Gioja, Linda. *Surfing the Edge of Chaos.* New York: Three Rivers Press, 2000.

Photo Removed Due to Copyright Restrictions

Figure 7: Operation Reframing Toward the Strategic Aim[137]

Operational conditions are the consequences of actions and represent an intermediate step

between the current state and the strategic aim. In figure 7, these operational conditions, defined

by the designer, mark the intermediate frame. In this manner designers iterate through a series of

operations to achieve the strategic aim. Learning takes place within the boundaries of the rival

system and between the related elements of the rival and the system frame. The relationships

between the elements of the rival system and between the system and rival frames determine the

point(s) for the initiation of action.

KEEP YOUR FRIENDS CLOSE AND YOUR ENEMIES CLOSER

Related elements within the nuclear-armed Iran system and rival frames include global

economic growth and stability, regional stability and security, the presence of sources outside of

Iran for weapons grade uranium and plutonium, the financial and logistical support needed for a

terrorist group to acquire, transport, and build a nuclear weapon, and the global presence of

Hezbollah with IRGC support. These elements present a variety of risks including the stability of

---

[137] Naveh, Shimon BG (res) Dr. *Questions of Operational Art, the Depth Structure of SOD.* Operational Theory Research Institute, December 2005, p. 16.

the global oil markets, regional stability through an emboldened Iran believing the regime is protected by the possession of nuclear weapons, further proliferation of nuclear technology and material by Iran through its support of terrorism, a ballistic missile threat to Europe, the GCC states, Central Asia and Israel, and finally to the US homeland through the IRGC, Hezbollah or other Iranian supported group.

In an effort to manage these risks, the US interests listed in figure 5 serve to define the strategic aims with securing the homeland from attack on top of the list. Efforts to promote global economic growth play on the demographic tensions faced by the government in Tehran. Pursuing regional stability by engaging the EU and GCC countries combined with nuclear deterrence puts Tehran between a desire for regional hegemony and the modern realities of the international balance of power. At the same time efforts to discover the structure and behavior of the various nuclear black market networks as well as the networks used to finance and support Hezbollah and other Iranian supported groups enables the disruption and destruction of these groups.

With these aims in mind the current path, or logic, of events between Iran, the UN, the EU-3, Russia, China and America is one of diplomatic stalemate at best due to the significant economic interest involved and direct military confrontation between Iran and America at worst. The eventual result, since the genie is already out of the bottle, is a nuclear-armed Iran, hardened positions on both sides, a high level of geo-political risk in the oil markets and an uncertain security situation in the region vis-à-vis Iran, Israel and the GCC states; an outcome that does not serve the strategic aims. Systemic change of both the system and rival frames through a series of operational frames is the goal.

Clearly, the strategic aims are not achievable overnight. Arguably, since Iran is the largest state supporter of terrorism, the current situation is part of the Long War against terrorism. In that sense the time horizon for a series of operations to achieve the strategic aims is likely measured in decades rather than months or even a few years. In terms of space, operations may cover a mountain valley in South America or multiple continents depending on the nature of the effort. Most importantly, the operations must be structured to observe and learn about the rival system. Figure 8 shows the strategic aims and end conditions for an initial operational frame.

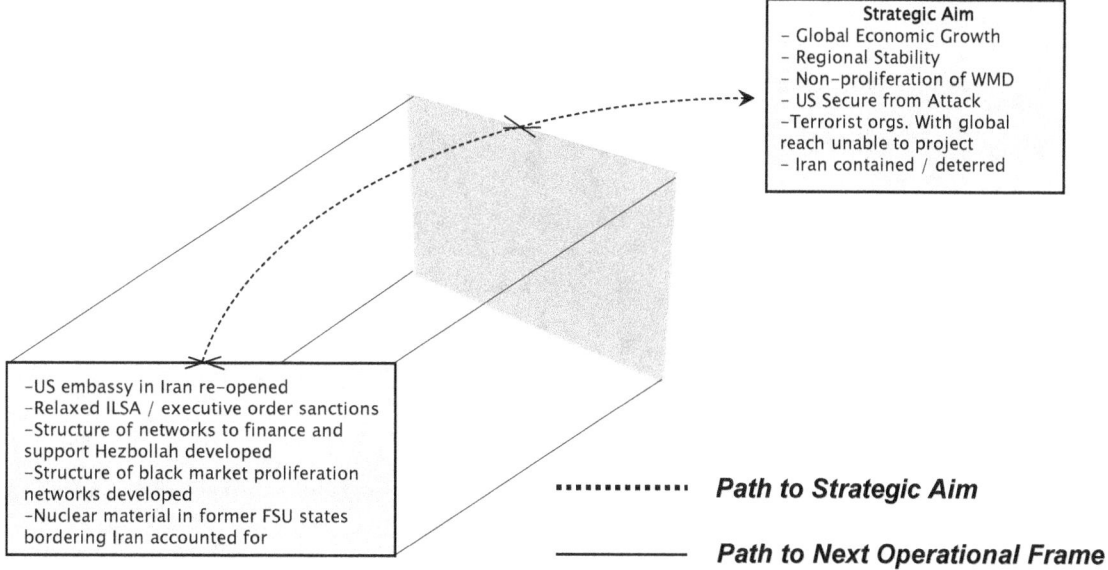

Figure 8: Strategic Aim with Initial Operational End Conditions

To achieve systemic change will take time but perhaps the most significant systemic change would be to reopen the US Embassy in Tehran: without any preconditions. The US and its allies did not win the Cold War without embassies in the "Evil Empire" and other eastern European countries. Having an embassy in one of the "Axis of Evil" countries that is open for business, in particular business with Iranian merchants and the younger generation presents a different view of America than seen in government propaganda and potentially exacerbates the government's demographic disadvantage. The request to reopen the embassy is also a way of recognizing the national pride present in the population, particularly the younger generation. This is not a carrot and stick approach or a grand bargain. In other words, the reopening of the embassy is not a carrot offered in return for something from Tehran; just offer to reopen the embassy. It is entirely possible Tehran would say no. Refusing the offer would potentially cause Tehran problems internationally with the UN, Russia, China and Europe. Tehran would almost certainly try to use such a request to their advantage with the population, but the potential positive impact over time would be worth it.

For a new embassy to be open for business there would need to be business to conduct. Relaxing the sanctions put in place by executive order and the Iran-Libya Sanctions Act would clear the way. This is different from the Cold War approach of strangling the Soviet economy but the information age has changed the economic landscape. A better model may be the current economic relationships with China. While Iran will not be the economic juggernaut China has become, reestablishing the embassy and getting back to business can serve to put the ruling clerics in between an economically improving population on one hand and increasing unemployment as the population comes of age on the other.

Maneuvering to better understand the tensions between the Iranian government, economy and people keeps the enemy closer. Maneuvering to understand the structure of the networks that support black market proliferation of nuclear components along with those used by Hezbollah to finance and support its operations are geared to eventually strangle them. First learning how these networks are structured is necessary before action can be taken against them. The time horizon in this effort is difficult because certain parts of the networks will emerge before others and raids will cause the network to change. That said actively operating against these networks from a warfighting viewpoint would systemically change the systems that enable Iran and Hezbollah to finance and support terrorism as well as benefit from the proliferation of nuclear components.

In the realm of nuclear components, particularly nuclear material, efforts are already underway to secure weapons useable material in Russia. The National Nuclear Security Administration, part of the Department of Energy, has been in a cooperative program with Russia for 10 years to secure vulnerable nuclear sites in Russia. Many smaller sites have been secured and the program is scheduled to be completed in 2008. If the sites within the former Soviet states closest to the Iranian border have not been secured then securing these sites needs to be accomplished to limit the availability of weapons usable material in relatively close proximity to the border.[138] Each of these end conditions for the operational frame is accomplished through different actions. From a military standpoint, will raiding as defined through systemic operational design be an effective?

STRATEGIC RAIDING – AN EFFECTIVE TOOL?

A strategic raid is "a self-contained act executed by self-sufficient elements within the context of the operational design." The purpose of a raid is to change the system and provide the opportunity to learn more about the system in order to progress toward a strategic aim. Colin Gray defines strategic utility as "the contribution of a particular kind of military activity to the course and outcome of an entire conflict."[139] The effectiveness of a given raid is subjective and often susceptible to a short term, tactical view.

However, the impact of a raid may not manifest itself for an extended period. To that end one way to assess the effectiveness of raids is to ask, "Is the rival system behavior moving toward the larger goal of the strategic aim?"[140] In that sense, while a single raid is designed to change the rival system, the strategic result is produced over time through a series of operations (operational frames) as the rival system changes to a state that meets the goal of the strategic aim. Therefore raiding within the SOD construct is effective provided the conditions of the rival system become more favorable relative to the strategic aim.

CONCLUSIONS

The Islamic Republic of Iran has pursued a nuclear program since 1985. Historically, the glory of the Persian Empire is distant but still real and for over 200 years, Iran has balanced the

---

[138] *NNSA Expands Nuclear Security Cooperation With Russia.* National Nuclear Security Administration Fact Sheet, October 2005.

[139] Gray, Colin S. *Explorations in Strategy.* Westport: Greenwood Press, 1996.

[140] Checkland, Peter and Scholes, Jim. *Soft Systems Methodology in Action.* West Sussex: John Wiley and Sons Ltd., 1990.

influence of one foreign power with another while always attempting to rid the country of outside influence. Today the balancing mechanism is nuclear energy. Building a series of nuclear reactors over the next decade with the help of Russia and within NPT guidelines will enable the IRI to benefit from the demand for fossil fuels by the growing economies of the world. Further, it is apparent the IRI will not operate like a Western democracy when dealing with other nations and can, if provoked, pose a threat to these democracies through its continuing ideological and financial support of terrorism through Hamas, Islamic Jihad, and Hezbollah. Finally, controlling the nuclear fuel cycle indigenously is a way to free the IRI from perceived foreign influence and promote the view of a resurgent Persian society, perhaps the leading society in Southwest Asia. The nuclear pursuits of the IRI also protect the regime, particularly if weapons are fielded. To that end, a deal that does not allow for a complete nuclear fuel cycle in Iran is unlikely.

By February of 2006, Tehran has what it needs to produce a weapon. While additional assistance from other countries or the black market might speed up the timeline, preventing Iran from being able to field a nuclear weapon if it wants to is no longer realistic. With a complete fuel cycle, the nuclear genie is out of the bottle and it is no longer possible to prevent Iran from fielding a weapon when it wants to. The two other categories within the technical capability required, a bomb design and technical training, are already complete thanks to international assistance.

Combined with IRI's history of support for terrorism its burgeoning nuclear program poses new and significant risk to US interests. While destroying many of the facilities within the IRI program is certainly possible and would likely set the program back, it is not likely to shut the program down and will serve as a unifying factor within Iran. The grand bargain, much like the current negotiations, requires the IRI to give up the nuclear fuel cycle and is therefore unlikely. New risks to the global economy, regional stability, proliferation of nuclear capability, and to the American homeland all point toward the need for renewed operational design to manage these risks.

Systemic Operational Design provides a methodology to manage the dynamic complexity of these new risks by synthesizing the Iranian historical pattern of balancing one foreign power with another while simultaneously seeking to limit foreign influence with the Western perspectives of international politics and the technical realities of Iran's nuclear program. A design that seeks to "Keep our friends close and our enemies closer" by simultaneously pursuing economic growth and regional stability through reopening of the US embassy in Iran while disrupting the foreign networks that support the proliferation of nuclear technology along with those that finance and support the foreign activities of Iran's IRGC and Hezbollah provides an initial frame and direction for action to manage these risks. Beyond the initial frame, systemic operational design provides a structure for the designer to progress through a series of operations to a state consistent with the strategic aims of global economic growth, regional stability and a secure homeland.

BIBLIOGRAPHY

AFP. "Iran May Have Handed Over Nuclear Core Plan by Accident." 20 November 2005. *Khaleej Times Online*, www.khaleejtimes.com, accessed 16 February 2006.

AFP. "Japan to Develop Iran Oilfield." *AlJazeera.net*, www.english.aljazeera.net, accessed 15 February 2006.

Allison, Graham. *Nuclear Terrorism, the Ultimate Preventable Catastrophe.* New York: Owl Books, Henry Holt and Company, 2005.

Associated Press. "Iran's Nuclear Plant Operating Full Swing." *The Jerusalem Post,* online edition, 11 August 2005. www.jpost.com.

Associated Press. "Iran to Resume Nuke Program in Face of Referral to UN Security Council," Foxnews.com, 4 February 2006. www.foxnews.com, accessed 4 February 2005.

Baker, Peter. "Putin's Concessions to U.S. are Limited the Bottom Line, Russia Unyielding on Iran Nuclear Project," *The Washington Post*, 16 August 2002.

Bowen, Wyn Q. and Kidd, Joanna. "The Iranian Nuclear Challenge." *International Affairs* 80, 2 (2004) 257-276.

Boureston, Jack and Ferguson, Charles D. "Schooling Iran's Atom Squad." *Bulletin of the Atomic Scientists*, May/June 2004 (vol. 60, no. 03), pp.31-35

Broad, William J. and Sanger, David E. "The Laptop. Relying on Computer, U.S. seeks to Prove Iran's Nuclear Aims." *The New York Times.* 13 November 2005

Busch, Nathan E. *No End in Sight, the Continuing Menace of Nuclear Proliferation.* Lexington: The University Press of Kentucky, 2004.

Byman, Daniel. "Should Hezbollah Be Next?" *Foreign Affairs*, Nov/Dec 2003. New York: Council on Foreign Relations, 2003

Checkland, Peter and Scholes, Jim. *Soft Systems Methodology in Action.* West Sussex: John Wiley and Sons Ltd., 1990

Chubin, Shahram. "Does Iran Want Nuclear Weapons?" *Survival*, Spring 1995. London: International Institute for Strategic Studies, 1995.

Cirincione, Joseph, Wolfsthal, Jon B., and Rajkumar, Miriam. *Deadly Arsenals, Nuclear, Biological and Chemical Threats.* 2nd Ed. Washington, D.C.: Carnegie Endowment for International Peace, 2005.

Coleman, Denise Youngblood, Editor in Chief. *Iran, 2005 Country Review.* Houston: Country Watch, Inc. 2005.

de Bellaigue, Christopher. "Iran" *Foreign Policy*, May/June 2005. Washington, D.C.: Carnegie Endowment for International Peace, 2005, pp. 18-24.

Eisenstadt, Michael. "Living with a Nuclear Iran?" *Survival*, Autumn 1999. London: International Institute for Strategic Studies, 1999.

Fahmy, Nabil. "Prospects for Arms Control and Proliferation in the Middle East." *The Nonproliferation Review*, Summer 2001, 1-7.

Freedman, Robert O. "Israel and the Threat from Iran's Nuclear Program." *Midstream* 51.2 (March-April 2005): 17 (3). *Expanded Academic ASAP*. Thompson Gale. US Air Force. 19 July 2005. Theodor Herzl Foundation, 2005

Frye, Richard N. *The Heritage of Persia.* Cleveland: The World Publishing Company, 1963

Glick, Caroline. "Column One: The Mullah's Moment in the Sun." *The Jerusalem Post.* 11 August 2005.

Grant, Rebecca. "Osirak and Beyond," *AIR FORCE Magazine*, August 2002, pp. 74-78.

Gray, Colin S. *Explorations in Strategy.* Westport: Greenwood Press, 1996.

Groseclose, Elgin. *Introduction to Iran.* New York: Oxford University Press, 1947.

Hoffman, Bruce. *Commando Raids: 1946-1983.* Santa Monica: RAND, 1985.

Hibbs, Mark. "Iran Told IAEA it Will Build Chinese UF6 Plant at Isfahan," *NuclearFuel*, 16 December 1996, pp. 10-11.

Implementation of the NPT Safeguards Agreement in the Islamic Republic of Iran. International Atomic Energy Agency, 18 November 2005

In Depth, Nuclear Fuel Cycle. BBC News, UK Edition. http://news.bbc.co.uk/2/hi/in_depth/world/2003/nuclear_fuel_cycle/mining/default.stm, accessed 28 October 2005

"Intellectuals Support Nuclear Drive." *Iran Daily.* 15 August 2005.

"Iran Stands like a Mountain in Pursuing its Nuclear Rights: Leader," *Tehran Times*, 20 August 2005. www.tehrantimes.com, accessed 21 Aug 05.

Joint Publication 1-02. *Department of Defense Dictionary of Military and Associated Terms*, 12 April 2001 as amended through 31 August 2005.

Jones, Peter. "Iran's Threat Perceptions and Arms Control Policies." *The Nonproliferation Review*, Fall 1998, 39-55.

Karimi, Nasser. "Iran Seeks Nuclear Fuel Guarantee," *Philadelphia Inquirer*, 28 November 2005.

Katouzian, Homa. "Mosaddeq's Government in Iranian History, Arbitrary Rule, Democracy, and the 1953 Coup." *Mohammad Mosaddeq and the 1953 Coup in Iran.* Gasiorowski, Mark J. and Byrne, Malcom, editors. Syracuse: Syracuse University Press, 2004, pp. 4-5.

Koch, Andrew and Wolf, Jeanette. "Iran's Nuclear Procurement Program: How Close to the Bomb?" *The Nonproliferation Review*, Fall 1997, 123-135.

Lenczowski, George, editor. *Iran under the Pahlavis.* Stanford: Hoover Institution Press, 1978.

Levite, Ariel E. and Sherwood-Randall, Elizabeth. "The Case for Discriminate Force." *Survival*, Winter 2002-03. London: International Institute for Strategic Studies, 2002.

Levitt, Matthew A. *Islamic Extremism in Europe*, FDCH Congressional Testimony, 27 April 2005, House International Relations Committee

Lieggi, Stephanie and Butler, Kenley. "The Globalization of Nuclear Smuggling: Methods Used by Two Pakistan-Based Networks." *NIS Export Control Observer*, May 2005. Monterey: Monterey Institute of International Studies, 2005.

Litwak, Robert S. "The New Calculus of Pre-emption." *Survival*, Winter 2002-03. London: International Institute for Strategic Studies, 2002.

Locy, Toni. "U.S. Looks at Potential Danger from Hezbollah," *USA Today*, 14 May 2003

Lutwak, Edward, Canby, Steven and Thomas, David. *A Systematic Review of "Commando" (Special) Operations 1939-1980.* Potomac: C&L Associates, 1982.

McKenna, Ted. "Chain Reaction. What Military Might Does Iran Have, and How Might it Use it?" *JED, The Journal of Electronic Defense*, July 2005. Horizon House Publications, 2005.

Mearsheimer, John J. *The Tragedy of Great Power Politics.* New York: W. W. Norton and Company, 2001.

Mehdi, Moslem. *Factional Politics in Post-Khomeini Iran.* Syracuse: Syracuse University Press, 2002.

MEIB Staff. "Hezbollah and the West African Diamond Trade," *Middle East Intelligence Bulletin*, June/July 2004, Vol. 6 Issue 6/7, pp. 6-8.

Metz, Helen Chapin, Editor. *Iran, a Country Study.* Washington, D.C.: Federal Research Division, Library of Congress, 1989.

Moaveni, Azadeh. "Storm in a Teacup," *Al –Ahram Weekly*, Issue 721, 16-22 December 2004. http://weekly.ahram.org.eg/2004/721/re6.htm, accessed 16 February 2006.

Morland, Howard. "The H-bomb Secret, to Know How is to Ask Why." *The Progressive.* November 1979, p. 3-12.

National Defense Strategy of the United States of America, March 2005.

National Strategy for Combating Terrorism, February 2003

National Strategy to Combat Weapons of Mass Destruction, December 2002

National Strategy for Homeland Security, July 2002.

National Security Strategy of the United States of America, September 2002

Naveh, Shimon BG (res) Dr. *In Pursuit of Military Excellence. The Evolution of Operational Theory.* London: Frank Cass Publishers, 1997.

Naveh, Shimon BG (res) Dr. *Questions of Operational Art, the Depth Structure of SOD.* Operational Theory Research Institute, December 2005.

NNSA Expands Nuclear Security Cooperation With Russia. National Nuclear Security Administration Fact Sheet, October 2005

"Nuclear Decision Depends on EU Approach." *Iran Daily.* 14 August 2005.

Pascale, Richard T., Millemann, Mark and Gioja, Linda. *Surfing the Edge of Chaos.* New York: Three Rivers Press, 2000.

Patterns of Global Terrorism 2003. Washington, D.C.: United States Department of State, April 2004

Perkovich, George. "For Tehran, Nuclear Program Is a Matter of National Pride." *Yale Global*, March 21, 2005. Washington, D.C.: Carnegie Endowment for International Peace, 2005.

Perkovich, George and Manzanero, Silvia. "Iran Gets the Bomb – Then What?" *Getting Ready for a Nuclear-Armed Iran.* Sololski, Henry and Clawson, Patrick editors. Carlisle: Strategic Studies Institute.

Pipes, Daniel. "The Hezbollah in America," *National Review*, 28 August 2000, Vol. 52 issue 16, p. 33.

Pollack, Kenneth M. *The Persian Puzzle, the Conflict Between Iran and America*. New York: Random House Trade Paperback Edition, 2005.

Pollack, Kenneth and Takeyh, Ray. "Taking on Tehran." *Foreign Affairs*, March/April 2005. New York: Council on Foreign Relations, 2005.

Rak, Claire. "The Role of Preventive Strikes in Counterproliferation Strategy: Two Case Studies." *Strategic Insight*. Monterey: Center for Contemporary Conflict, 2003.

Reuters. "Iran in Gas Deal with European Firms." *AlJazeera.net*, www.english.aljazeera.net, accessed 25 February 2006.

Senge, Peter M. *The Fifth Discipline, the Art & Practice of the Learning Organization*. New York: Doubleday, 1990.

Serber, Robert. *The Los Alamos Primer. The First Lectures on How to Build an Atomic Bomb*. Berkeley: University of California Press, 1992.

Snyder, Jack. "One World, Rival Theories." *Foreign Policy*, November/December 2004. Washington, D.C.: Carnegie Institute for International Peace, 2004. pp. 53-62.

Sorrells, William, Downing, Glen R., Blakesley, Paul J., Pendhall, David W., Walk, Jason K. and Wallwork, Richard D. *Systemic Operational Design: An Introduction*. Unpublished monograph. School of Advanced Military Studies, US Army Command and General Staff College, AY 04-05.

Southworth, Samuel A., editor. *Great Raids in History; From Drake to Desert One*. New York: Sarpedon, 1997.

Squassoni, Sharon A. *Weapons of Mass Destruction: Trade between North Korea and Pakistan*. Washington, D.C.: Congressional Research Service, 11 March 2004, p. 11

"Students Form Human Chain Around Isfahan UCF." *Tehran Times*, 17 August 2005.

Taheri, Amir. "Eye of the Storm: Behind the Scenes in Tehran." *The Jerusalem Post.* 15 August 2005.

United States Special Operations Command Mission, US Special Operations Command, http://www.socom.mil/Docs/Command_Mission-060214.pdf, accessed 19 February 2006.

U.S. Congress, Office of Technology Assessment. *Technologies Underlying Weapons of Mass Destruction*, OTA-BP-ISC-115. Washington, D.C.: U.S. Government Printing Office, December 1993.

US Strategic Command SNAP SHOT, US Strategic Command, February 2006, http://www.stratcom.mil/fact_sheets/SnapShot.doc, accessed 19 February 2006.

Venter, Al J. *Iran's Nuclear Option, Tehran's Quest for the Atom Bomb*. Havertown: Casemate Publishers, 2005.

Yaphe, Judith S. and Lutes, Charles D. *Reassessing the Implications of a Nuclear Armed Iran, McNair Paper 69*. Washington, D.C.: National Defense University, 2005.

Yapp, M.E. *The Making of the Modern Near East*, 1792-1923. New York: Longman, Inc., 1987

Yapp, M.E. *The Near East Since the First World War*. New York: Longman, Inc. 1991

Zahedi, Ardeshir. "Iran's Nuclear Ambitions." *Wall Street Journal*, 25 June 2004

www.ingramcontent.com/pod-product-compliance
Lightning Source LLC
Chambersburg PA
CBHW080535290526
45790CB00006B/2411